A Strong Relationship With God

By Jeffrey Kobman

This book is dedicated to my father and mother, Donald and Virginia Kobman. They stuck with me when I was in rebellion and fighting God. I have grown into a man because of their love, guidance, kindness and the redemptive work of my God. Thank you, Mom and Dad, and above all thank you Lord.

For all of this, I am forever grateful. In Jesus precious name. Amen.

Jeffrey Kobman
Spotsylvania, Virginia
January 2022

Quote taken from *My Utmost for His Highest* by Oswald Chambers, edited by James Reimann, © 1992 by Oswald Chambers Publications Assn., Ltd. Used by permission of Our Daily Bread Publishing, Grand Rapids MI 49501. All rights reserved.

Bible Copyrights

The following versions of the Bible were used in this book. The author wishes to thank the Bible translators for their diligence in assembling these versions of the Holy Bible to bring glory to God.

KJV - King James Version
Scripture quotations marked "KJV" are taken from the Holy Bible, King James Version, Cambridge, 1769.

NLT - New Living Translation
Scripture quotations marked "NLT" are taken from the Holy Bible, New Living Translation, copyright 1996. Used by permission of Tyndale House Publishers, Inc., Wheaton, Illinois 60189. All rights reserved.

NIV - New International Version
Scripture quotations marked "NIV" are taken from HOLY BIBLE, NEW INTERNATIONAL VERSION. Copyright 1973, 1978, 1984 by International Bible Society. Used by permission of Zondervan Publishing House.

MSG – The Message
Scripture taken from *THE MESSAGE*. Copyright © 1993, 1994, 1995, 1996, 2000, 2001, 2002. Used by permission of NavPress Publishing Group.

ESV - The Holy Bible: English Standard Version
Scripture quotations marked "ESV" are taken from The Holy Bible: English Standard Version, copyright 2001, Wheaton: Good News Publishers. Used by permission. All rights reserved.

AMP - The Amplified Bible
Scripture quotations marked "The Amplified Bible" or "The Amplified New Testament" are taken from The Amplified Bible, Old Testament copyright 1965, 1987 by the Zondervan Corporation and The Amplified New Testament copyright 1958, 1987 by The Lockman Foundation. Used by permission. All rights reserved.

Table of Contents

Chapter One	7
Chapter Two	31
Chapter Three	51
Chapter Four	71
Chapter Five	95
Chapter Six	119
Chapter Seven	149
Chapter Eight	167
Chapter Nine	187
Chapter Ten	203

PLEASE share this book with someone after you read it – THANKS!!

Chapter 1

Why Hebrews?

Hebrews is a book of the relationship between God and man. It is written to all people, Hebrews and Gentiles alike. This epistle is just as relevant today as it was when it was written, probably in the first century.

The central message in the four Gospels is a message of redemption. For the Son of Man came to seek and save those who are lost. (Luke 19:10 NIV) God wants all people everywhere to come home to Him. He is not angry, so "please come home to God." When we read and understand the book of Hebrews, we can use this phrase concerning the Gospels, "come home and have a relationship with God." Jesus came to bring people home to His Father, our heavenly Father.

Jesus came to earth and brought the Gospel (the Good News) to us. He had a relationship with the Father and wanted us to know the <u>great</u> <u>news</u> that God wanted a relationship with us. He did not send Jesus to condemn us to eternal death, He was sent to save us and bring us home. It now became entirely possible for us to have that relationship with God. Jesus told us that

> I am the way and the truth and the life. No one comes to the Father except through me. (John 14:6 NIV)

Another way to say this is *it's impossible to approach and get to God without Jesus.* Nobody gets to the Father for an eternal, holy relationship with God without Jesus Christ. This is a simple but profound truth. All of the religious exercises, rituals and complicated formulas that are created by people will not get you to God. Nobody but Jesus can "hook you up" with God because no amount of hard work and service for God works.

Why Hebrews? The letter to the Hebrews talks about our relationship with the Father which is guaranteed by Jesus. This was because of His sacrifice on the cross and His resurrection from the dead. Because of the Gospels, we can clearly see all of the torture and suffering that Jesus endured. This was all God's plan to sacrifice His Son for the sins of the people.

> But God clearly shows *and* proves His own love for us, by the fact that while we were still sinners, Christ died for us. *(Romans 5:8 AMP)*

This sacrifice of Christ by the Father brings us the offer so that we can establish and develop a relationship with God. What a great and wonderful opportunity – through Jesus Christ we can approach and have a personal relationship with almighty God! We were separated from God and are now invited and escorted home to God.

Society today is splintered and divided over a many different issues – politics, religion, the economy, global warming and others. As it was in times past and is still true today, the only answer to these problems for all people is turning to God through His Son Jesus Christ. God is the only one who can bring resolution to these important, "hot-button" issues by changing people from the inside out. This only solution and resolution of the issues that affect people comes through His redemption and God is the only one who has the ability to redeem the people of this world. Through this redemption, we approach God and are invited to come home. This is the significance of turning to God through Jesus.

People have tried a variety of temporary fixes to solve the many challenges that face society. When one so-called "fix" is offered to solve the world's problems, it becomes popular. Soon it is shown as an ineffective "fix it" measure that fails in one way or another. Each time a new controversy arises, another so-called answer is given – "try this" or "try that." This floats around in the public forum of the social media, television and public opinion. The only real, lasting answer is turn to God through Jesus. These ineffective suggestions are never-ending and just don't work. Jesus is the only way to solve the myriad of issues. God will transform a challenging problem into a sure, unchangeable solution.

The book of Hebrews addresses the questions and problems that the Hebrews who had become

Christians were faced with. Some had questions concerning their faith in Christ and some were returning to actively follow the Law. The people's problems were found in these basic questions - "Is Christ the way to God or should we return to following and keeping the Law of Moses?" "Is the Law able to save me or should I trust only in Christ?" "Is Jesus really the way to God?" The author of Hebrews dealt with these issues at length and answered these questions.

The questions about our relationship with Christ that the people were asking were clearly answered by establishing and nurturing a relationship with God. Everyone enters the Christian life by means of a personal relationship with Jesus Christ. The song by Andrae Crouch tells us

> Jesus is the answer for the world today
> Above Him there's no other, Jesus is the way.
> (*Jesus Is the Answer* © Bud-john Songs, Inc.)

These believers needed to know that a relationship with Jesus Christ is better than a return to living under the Law. A friend told me that one way to look at Hebrews is that "Jesus is mo' better." This is exactly right. A relationship with God through Jesus Christ is better, more superior and more desirable than a relationship under the Law. There are many reasons that this relationship is *better*. The two reasons are that this relationship with God is *perfect* and it is *eternal*, because God is perfect and eternal.

Why Hebrews? We saw that Hebrews teaches us that our relationship with God is *better, perfect* and *eternal*. It is *perfect* because our perfect God makes us perfect - we are in Him and are made a part of Him.

> This God - his way is perfect; the word of the LORD proves true; he is a shield for all those who take refuge in him. (Psalm 18:30 ESV)
>
> For by that one offering he forever made perfect those who are being made holy. (Hebrews 10:14 NLT)
>
> You therefore must be perfect, as your heavenly Father is perfect. (Matthew 5:48 ESV)
>
> This God - his way is perfect; the word of the LORD proves true; he is a shield for all those who take refuge in him. (2 Samuel 22:31 ESV)

His way is perfect and believers enter into a relationship with our perfect God.

Our relationship with God is *eternal* because God through Jesus Christ bought our redemption which is seen in John 3:16. Eternal life was always God's plan. Adam and Eve were created to live eternally in a relationship with God. But they broke the relationship through sin. It took a perfect sacrifice to restore man's eternal relationship with God.

The sacrifice that Jesus brought to the cross of Himself was far superior to the animals that the priests sacrificed in the Old Testament. The priests were human and brought sacrifices that were meant to be a temporary "covering" for sin, not a permanent elimination of sin. Jesus brought a perfect sacrifice which totally eradicated and eliminated sin forever. This was available for everyone who would choose to believe.

> For God's will was for us to be made holy by the sacrifice of the body of Jesus Christ, once for all time. Under the old covenant, the priest stands and ministers before the altar day after day, offering the same sacrifices again and again, which can never take away sins. But our High Priest offered himself to God as a single sacrifice for sins, good for all time. (Hebrews 10:10-12a NLT)
>
> For Christ also suffered once for sins, the righteous for the unrighteous, to bring you to God. (1 Peter 3:18a NIV)

Hebrews is a link between the Old Testament, the four Gospels and the life that we live today in Christ. Hebrews joins together the Messiah coming to earth to rescue mankind and our establishing a relationship with Christ as Savior and Lord.

In the Old Testament, we see relationship the prophets and servants of God had with God. Jonah had a relationship but tried hard to avoid God. God told him to go to Nineveh and proclaim God's judgement so the people would repent before God.

Jonah boarded a ship and traveled in the opposite direction so he could get away from God. (Jonah 1:3) In contrast, the prophet Jeremiah had a relationship with God that was one of obedience. Jeremiah preached the truth that God gave him to bring to the people. As a result of obeying God, Jeremiah suffered many things and fulfilled what God wanted him to do.

Jonah and Jeremiah worked through some big problems. These two prophets as well as many others encountered tough situations in their lives. Big and small challenges and problems are normal for those who trust God. In all of this we keep our relationship of faith in God active and keep our hope alive. Our Lord was resurrected and He now gives us His life and hope. We are <u>in Him</u>.

Even though believers have problems and challenges, Jesus the Messiah suffered for each of us. We were the object of His love while He suffered. The sacrifice of Jesus was a perfect sacrifice and a better sacrifice. Jesus suffered, died and rose from the dead for every believer. God invites those who do not believe to enter His suffering and death.

> He said to them, "How foolish you are, and how slow to believe all that the prophets have spoken! Did not the Messiah have to suffer these things and then enter his glory?" And beginning with Moses and all the Prophets, he explained to them what was said in all the Scriptures concerning himself. (Luke 25.24-27 NIV)

We do not know exactly what Jesus explained to them, but we know that He spoke about the Messianic scriptures from Moses and the prophets in the Old Testament.

One day in Nazareth, Jesus stood up in the synagogue and read the scriptures. He focused on a scripture in Isaiah.

> The Spirit of the Lord GOD is upon me; because the LORD hath anointed me to preach good tidings unto the meek; he hath sent me to bind up the brokenhearted, to proclaim liberty to the captives, and the opening of the prison to them that are bound; To proclaim the acceptable year of the LORD (Isaiah 61:1-2a KJV)

> The Spirit of the Sovereign LORD is upon me, for the LORD has anointed me
> to bring good news to the poor. He has sent me to comfort the brokenhearted and to proclaim that captives will be released and prisoners will be freed. He has sent me to tell those who mourn that the time of the LORD's favor has come (Isaiah 61:1-2a NLT)

Jesus' reading Isaiah in the synagogue was also recorded in Luke 4. He was telling the people in the synagogue that He was the Messiah and that He came to bring God's good news to meek people, those who were needy, poor, humble and afflicted. He came to help those who are shattered, broken, crushed, maimed, crippled, and wrecked. Liberty (freedom) was proclaimed by Jesus to those who were captive. He brought the "acceptable year of the Lord" to people. The NLT calls it the time of God's favor. In the Hebrew language, it means goodwill and acceptance.

The coming of Jesus the Messiah was a special visitation that brought the kingdom of God close to people. It was the perfect time to enter into a relationship with God. God sent Jesus to rescue people from their tragic lives. He was there and ready to receive them. This same special favor and visitation from God is here today. He sent Jesus. This is the eternal promise from God.

This day in the synagogue was similar to when Jesus taught about the Parable of the Good Samaritan. (Luke 10:30-37) Jesus used the mercy shown by the Samaritan as an example to teach the people about the wonderful mercy of God. Charles Spurgeon said, "God's mercy is so great that you may sooner drain the sea of its water, or deprive the sun of its light, or make space too narrow, than diminish the great mercy of God." The Samaritan demonstrated mercy and we should extend mercy to those who need it. The mercy of God is available to all.

The people in the synagogue who heard Jesus read Isaiah that day did not comprehend the true nature of their lives. They had been "beaten and robbed" by the devil. They were in held by many afflictions – they were sick, diseased, bound up, confined to a virtual prison and crippled by their sin. They were separated from God. This was all because they needed what Jesus offered to them – a relationship with God. Jesus, the Messiah was there in the synagogue and they became furious at His proclamation! They immediately rejected Him and the good news of a new life that He brought. (Luke 4:28-30) The people were hardhearted and rejected God, just as their ancestors had done.

> But because of your callous stubbornness and unrepentant heart you are [deliberately] storing up wrath for yourself on the day of wrath when God's righteous judgment will be revealed. (Romans 2:5 AMP)

People are faced with the same exact problem today – rejecting God. Across society, people keep rejecting Him. What they desperately need is to embrace God and begin a relationship with Him.

Jesus brought a better covenant that He makes with each of us and became the guarantor of this same better covenant. (Hebrews 7:22b NIV) Jesus offered this new life and does the same thing today.

When we see the English word *saved* in our Bibles, the Greek word is *sozo*. It means to keep safe and sound, rescue from danger, destruction, injury or peril and to save the injured, diseased by healing and restoration. This includes a more traditional understanding of *salvation* – saved from sin when we are washed in the blood of Jesus. *Sozo* is a comprehensive word that shows God's love for everyone. People rejected God's help in the Messiah and people still reject Him today.

A relationship with God is precious and available to all. Unbelievers can receive Him for the first time and believers can deepen and extend their relationship as they surrender, grow and strengthen themselves in God. He came to give us new life and that is exactly what He does for each of us.

That day in the Nazarene synagogue, the anointed Messiah came to visit and invite the Jews to come to Him and return to God. Today, the same anointed Messiah, Jesus Christ invites us to come home to God. Will you accept His personal ministry to you?

Jesus came and brought a new relationship with God that was not based on following and keeping the Law of Moses. Instead, if anyone accepts and receives a relationship with Christ, that person becomes a totally new creation. The old person dies and goes away and everything becomes a new creation. (2 Corinthians 5:17) God sent His Son into the world to rescue and save us, not to condemn us. People were already condemned to death because of sin and Jesus came to offer eternal life to all, and all we need to do is who receive Him. This is a simple but profound idea that is a reality.

> This is how much God loved the world: He gave his Son, his one and only Son. And this is why: so that no one need be destroyed; by believing in him, anyone can have a whole and

> lasting life. God didn't go to all the trouble of sending his Son merely to point an accusing finger, telling the world how bad it was. He came to help, to put the world right again. Anyone who trusts in him is acquitted; anyone who refuses to trust him has long since been under the death sentence without knowing it. And why? Because of that person's failure to believe in the one-of-a-kind Son of God when introduced to him. (John 3:16-18 MSG)

Hebrews emphasizes the superiority of Jesus' sacrifice and the life it brought to earth. His rescue, healing, deliverance, prosperity and salvation is our abundant life. On the other hand, the devil will steal, kill and destroy.

> The thief comes only to steal and kill and destroy; I have come that they may have life, and have it to the full. (John 10:10 NIV)

The Greek words for *steal, kill and destroy* are very revealing. *Steal* is to commit a theft by stealth – secretly, quietly and without you knowing. *Kill* is to slaughter and *destroy* is to render someone useless and then eliminate them. *Destroy* is to entirely make useless, to have eternal misery, to be lost or perish. All of these attacks are devastating. This alone is a great reason to run to Jesus to trust and walk with Him. In spite of these works of the devil, the alternative with Jesus is extraordinary. *Abundantly* in John 10:10 means a life that is over and above, more than necessary, exceeding, superadded and superior. The devil is completely evil and Jesus is totally good.

He is all-powerful, all-loving and has promised to protect and keep us. And, this *abundant life* is perfect. He is perfect and He acts on our behalf perfectly.

The righteousness that God gives to His saved people in a major theme in Hebrews. He gives this righteousness to us out of love for His children.

God appoints and makes us His ambassadors. He prepares and sends us to carry the message of His kingdom to others. Our message to the people of the world is "come home to God."

> We are therefore Christ's ambassadors, as though God were making his appeal through us. We implore you on Christ's behalf: Be reconciled to God. God made him who had no sin to be sin for us, so that in him we might become the righteousness of God. (2 Corinthians 5:20-21 NIV)

> So, we are ambassadors for Christ, as though God were making His appeal through us; we [as Christ's representatives] plead with you on behalf of Christ to be reconciled to God. He made Christ who knew no sin to [judicially] be sin on our behalf, so that in Him we would become the righteousness of God [that is, we would be made acceptable to Him and placed in a right relationship with Him by His gracious lovingkindness]. (2 Corinthians 5:20-21 AMP)

This reconciliation to God brings His righteousness to us when we are made right by God. This gives us the ability to have a relationship with God. It's not our ability, but it is God's righteousness. God invites and saves us. We simply receive it when we make Jesus the Lord of our life by faith. A life well-lived is one where we are reconciled to God and have a relationship with Him.

Jesus calls us friends, not servants. We develop a close friendship in our loving relationship with Him.

> I no longer call you servants, because a servant does not know his master's business. Instead, I have called you friends, for everything that I learned from my Father I have made known to you. (John 15:15 NIV)
>
> I'm no longer calling you servants because servants don't understand what their master is thinking and planning. No, I've named you friends because I've let you in on everything I've heard from the Father. (John 15:15 MSG)

We are made righteous by God and brought to God. This is done for His people as individuals and as a group. This is all done as a part of His relationship with us. We trust Him, we live in Him and we know Him.

This new relationship with God with us was spoken of by the prophet Isaiah.

> Forget the former things; do not dwell on the past. See, I am doing a new thing!
> Now it springs up; do you not perceive it? I am making a way in the wilderness

> and streams in the wasteland. (Isaiah 43:18-19 NIV)

The Lord is telling us that a new thing is coming and He will do it. God will provide "safe passage" for His people as we go through tough times and challenging situations. The new thing that God does will bring us a God-inspired, God-directed and God-ordained relationship. We go to God on His terms, not on the man-centered, uninspired relationship that religion brings.

> They will receive the LORD's blessing and have a right relationship with God their savior. (Psalm 24:5 NLT)

God gave the Law to the children of Israel after He miraculously brought them out of Egypt. Stephen Cole said that the Law was given "to reveal His standard of absolute righteousness to convict us all of our true guilt before Him." His Law would cause people to see their need for God. Nobody can get right with God by their own efforts - we need Christ.

God is perfect and His Law is perfect, but God gave His holy Law to imperfect people. Israel proved that this situation of living life as law-keepers would not work. Man is weak, morally undecided and if left alone would choose unbelief over God. They chose sin when they should have chosen God. God sent Jesus Christ the Messiah to Israel to rescue them from having to keep the Law to attempt to become righteous through obedience to the commandments. In spite of God's Law being perfect, man needed a better way. They needed the Messiah, the sent-one Jesus Christ.

> For on the one hand there is an annulling of the former commandment because of its weakness and unprofitableness, for the law made nothing perfect; on the other hand, *there is the* bringing in of a better hope, through which we draw near to God. (Hebrews 7:18-19 NKJV)

Hebrews was written to tell the Jews that God sent the Messiah Jesus Christ to rescue them from sin. It is easy for people to see themselves as being a "good person" but <u>everyone</u> has sinned. Jesus took care of the sin problem for eternity. He did it one time for all people. The Law made nothing perfect, but God sent a better hope for us to receive and live. The Law is holy. Man failed to keep the Law so it was an ineffective solution to forgiving sin and making man righteous. God sent Jesus as Savior, a better hope for us to follow.

People could now take the better hope and follow the perfect Christ. Our perfect God sent the perfect Savior to allow us to be redeemed and changed to live righteous for Him. We were made complete individuals, free from sin because of Christ. Living in the perfect man Jesus Christ is superior to an imperfect man living a life under the Law.

God calls us to obey the Gospel of Jesus Christ to bring us to God. God replaced the imperfect and ineffective system of the Law with a perfect and effective sacrifice – Jesus Christ. The prophet Samuel told King Saul that obeying God is always better than bringing an imperfect animal sacrifice to God. Man was faced with the unsolvable problem of needing a suitable sacrifice living under the Law.

> Does the LORD delight in burnt offerings and sacrifices as much as in obeying the LORD? To obey is better than sacrifice, and to heed is better than the fat of rams. (1 Samuel 15:22 NIV)

We learn from this verse that obedience to God is simply *better*. God is not looking for more and more animals sacrificed, He wants all people redeemed to Himself. Obeying God and following His good news (the Gospel) brings new life. God loves us and wants good things for us. But it must be on His terms – eternal life is only in Jesus Christ.

> This is how much God loved the world: He gave his Son, his one and only Son. And this is why: so that no one need be destroyed; by believing in him, anyone can have a whole and lasting life. God didn't go to all the trouble of sending his Son merely to point an accusing finger, telling the world how bad it was. He came to help, to put the world right again. (John 3:16-17a MSG)

Obeying God takes each of us using our faith intentionally. We must decide that we want a relationship with God and that we will obey God. We rely on God to empower us with His Holy Spirit. We should say – "Lord, help me to obey You!" God is a good God and is ready and willing to help us when we reach out to Him.

Because Jesus was 100% God and 100% man, we know that as a man He had to obey God. He always obeyed God and was a man without sin. He was sacrificed by the Father for us to pay for all of the sins of people, and specifically to pay for each of our sin.

> And having been perfected, He [Jesus] became the author of eternal salvation to all who obey Him, (Hebrews 5:9 NIV)

Because of this perfect sacrifice, we are made righteous and are given a wonderful relationship with Him.

The sacrifice that was presented to God in the Old Testament was given to God with obedience and humility. When Jesus was sacrificed, He presented Himself to God with obedience and humility. Jesus fully obeyed God.

> then He said, "BEHOLD, I HAVE COME TO DO YOUR WILL." [And so] He does away with the first [covenant as a means of atoning for sin based on animal sacrifices] so that He may inaugurate *and* establish the second [covenant by means of obedience]. (Hebrews 10:9 AMP)

Jesus presented His own blood to God for everyone to bring the second (new) covenant. Everyone can now be made right with God because of the sacrifice of Jesus. Why Hebrews? It tells the story of our redemption because of the act of sacrifice and obedience that Jesus Christ did for each of us.

Hebrews gives every Jew and Gentile hope. Hope in God is having confidence in God's ability and desire to help each of us. Even when we become worried, discouraged, lose all hope and are ready to give up, we can know the extremely encouraging truth - God will help us and God will help us.

> Why, my soul, are you downcast? Why so disturbed within me? Put your hope in God, for I will yet praise him, my Savior and my God. (Psalm 43:5 NIV)
>
> Why am I discouraged? Why is my heart so sad? I will put my hope in God! I will praise him again— my Savior and my God! (Psalm 43:5 NLT)

Our hope is in Him and we praise Him. God's desire is to help us. But believers have a responsibility – to hold on to our hope in God confidently. Our faith in God tells us that He will help us because He is faithful. Believers choose to trust God regardless of what goes on around them or the trouble that comes.

> Because of the LORD's great love, we are not consumed, for his compassions never fail. They are new every morning; great is your faithfulness. I say to myself, "The LORD is my

> portion; therefore, I will wait for him."
> (Lamentations 3:22-24 NIV)

> God's loyal love couldn't have run out, his merciful love couldn't have dried up.
> They're created new every morning. How great your faithfulness! I'm sticking with God (I say it over and over). He's all I've got left.
> (Lamentations 3:22-24 MSG)

Believers have a relationship with God. They run to God when discouragement comes and their courage fails. Believers run to God in hope knowing that "great is Your faithfulness to me." God will always keep the believer because of His relationship. He is faithful to His people because of His great love.

Jews had a covenant relationship with God, but for the Gentiles there was nothing. Gentiles were without hope and without God. No hope for God in their life and no access to God.

> remember that at that time you were separate from Christ, excluded from citizenship in Israel and foreigners to the covenants of the promise, without hope and without God in the world. But now in Christ Jesus you who once were far away have been brought near by the blood of Christ. (Ephesians 2:12-13 NIV)

Israel hoped in God but they served Him through the Law. Jesus came and willingly gave Himself to be sacrificed on the cross. Jew and Gentile alike could now be righteous before God. The relationship that

Jesus had with the Father was now available to everyone.

> I and the Father are one. (John 10:30 NIV)

> [Jesus said He will] give them eternal life, and they shall never perish; no one will snatch them out of my hand: My Father, who has given them to me, is greater than all; no one can snatch them out of my Father's hand. (John 10:28-29 NIV)

These words from Jesus are incredible and give us hope. We can live our lives knowing that a relationship with God through Jesus Christ is our promise. God brings us a relationship with Him – we now know God and His glory. It was not just Israel who would know God, it would now be available to all people.

> God wanted everyone, not just Jews, to know this rich and glorious secret inside and out, regardless of their background, regardless of their religious standing. The mystery in a nutshell is just this: Christ is in you, so therefore you can look forward to sharing in God's glory. It's that simple. (Colossians 1:27 MSG)

Our faith and hope brings us an indescribable gift from God – we don't earn or deserve it. We take hold of this gift tightly and hold on to it for our entire lives.

> God did this so that, by two unchangeable things in which it is impossible for God to lie, we who have fled to take hold of the hope set before us may be greatly encouraged. (Hebrews 3:18 NIV)
>
> We who have run for our very lives to God have every reason to grab the promised hope with both hands and never let go. (Hebrews 3:18 MSG)

Our relationship with Him brings us a lasting hope in God. We can say, "I confidently hope in God. I know that He will always come through." Righteous people live by faith because they are able to confidently hope in God.

> Let us hold unswervingly to the hope we profess, for he who promised is faithful. (Hebrews 10:23 NIV)
>
> Let us hold tightly without wavering to the hope we affirm, for God can be trusted to keep his promise. (Hebrews 10:23 NLT)

Why Hebrews? Hebrews offer a better opportunity for us as New Testament believers than the Jews had under the Law in the Old Testament. The Old Testament clearly showed the hope of the Messiah, but the promise was far off. Jesus brought us fulfillment to that promise.

> But God demonstrates his own love for us in this: While we were still sinners, Christ died for us. (Romans 5:8 NIV)

God loves us. God saw our need. God sent Jesus.

Chapter Questions

1. In your own words, write one sentence that explains to the reader, "Why Hebrews?" In other words, why is Hebrews significant or important to you?

2. Choose 1 or 2 scriptures from this chapter and explain why you enjoy these scriptures. Tell why they are meaningful to you.

3. Jesus was a "better sacrifice." Why is this true?

4. Describe why hope in Jesus is available to people.

5. Why do believers have hope?

6. Jesus was a perfect sacrifice. Why is this true?

7. The devil steals, kills and destroys. Explain one way that this happens when the devil attacks you.

8. On page 6, 2 Corinthians 5:20-22 calls believers "ambassadors." In what way(s) is a Christian an ambassador for Christ?

9. The Greek word *sozo* is on page 5. Using the text, briefly explain *sozo*.

10. On page 3, our relationship with God is *better, perfect* and *eternal*. Choose one of the 3 words and explain it.

Chapter 2

What Is A Relationship With God?

First, what is a relationship? It is a personal encounter with another person or group. A relationship often develops into a lasting connection. Some relationships are formal and some are casual. Family and friends are usually a more casual relationship than the more formal relationship we have with a boss, a school principal or a judge. Family relationships are established and often create a bond of loyalty. Even when a family is dysfunctional, a bond still exists – whether healthy or unhealthy.

Believers have a relationship with God that is a permanent and unbreakable. This is a wonderful relationship where He will never abandon us, but rather He will keep us close to Him like a mother hen gathers and protects her chicks. (Luke 13:34) This is God's concept of a permanent relationship. He will never get rid of us because every believer has a permanent bond with Him. This bond is eternal.

> God has said, "Never will I leave you; never will I forsake you." (Hebrews 13:5b NIV)

> He has said, "I will never [under any circumstances] desert you [nor give you up nor leave you without support, nor will I in any degree leave you helpless], Nor will I forsake, *or* let you down *or* relax My hold on you [assuredly not]!" (Hebrews 13:5b AMP)
>
> Since God assured us, "I'll never let you down, never walk off and leave you," we can boldly quote, God is there, ready to help; I'm fearless no matter what.
> Who or what can get to me? (Hebrews 13:5-6 MSG)

His bond is His promise in which He guarantees to keep us forever. His Word is true and available to all.

God is promising that He is not going somewhere else, "I will always be with you, always." Instead of worrying, let God's promise get ahold of you! Our relationship with Him is sure and secure – He won't get rid of us, it's guaranteed. We can be assured that our relationship with God is permanent, rich and holy.

This permanence is shown in the parable of the Vine and the Branches in John 15. God's plan and desire is for every believer to get attached and stay attached. When we remain "hooked up" with God, we grow and thrive in Him. This is our "forever" relationship with God. As a branch feeds from the vine, believers remain in their relationship which provides all of our needs and sustenance from God.

God provides all of our needs by means of His wealth. (Philippians 4:19) It is easy to focus on material things when we talk about His meeting our needs. God meets all of our needs in all of the areas of our lives. Jesus spoke of God's provision when he talked about how magnificently God cares for the birds and flowers. (Matthew 6) Jesus tells us to see this example of God's provision and to have confidence in His provision in our lives.

In our relationship with God, we enter into His rest. This means we depend upon Him like the birds and flowers. I will feed my birds and water my garden because I want to do this. The birds and garden do not need to fear that I will "abandon" them. Believers do not need to fear that God will abandon them – He will never get rid of me! His relationship with us is permanent.

Our responsibility in this relationship is to have faith in God and trust Him in the big and little things. This takes cooperation on our part. We work together with Him, both serving Him and receiving from Him. We keep a soft heart that is not hardened or a heart of unbelief. (Hebrews 3:12-15) Jesus said "I am the way..." (John 14:6) which means He is everything to us. We come to the Father through Jesus and our relationship is cemented – we are glued to Him forever. This is the nature of our relationship with God.

Hebrews tell us that our relationship with God through Jesus Christ is superior to a relationship with God through the Law. A relationship that is through the Law requires performance so that we earn God's blessings. People were required to do certain things and not do other things. Under the Law, we are required to bring sacrifices to God for our sins and as an act of worship. Our relationship with Jesus Christ is one of faith and we live in this relationship and obey God because we love Him. The Law requires obedience, but serving Jesus is a choice we make from a good heart and our free will. This is shown in the Law.

> You shall love the LORD your God with all your heart *and* mind and with all your soul and with all your strength [your entire being]. (Deuteronomy 6:5 AMP)

Jesus chose to love God in this way. He added to the scripture in Deuteronomy 6 that

> This is the first and greatest commandment. The second is like it, "You shall love your neighbor as yourself [that is, unselfishly seek the best or higher good for others].' The whole Law and the [writings of the] Prophets depend on these two commandments." (Matthew 22:38-40 AMP)

This is how I choose to love God. I love Him and I love other people. We are obeying God as we love Him and love the people around us – family, friends, acquaintances and strangers. This includes those who are easy to love as well as the unlovable.

God pursued Abraham and he responded to God with faith. When God told Abraham to "go from your present country" and go where God would tell him, he obeyed. This is Abraham's faith in action through obedience to God's wishes. We do not know what Abraham said, but we know he departed his home. Later he built an altar to God at Shechem and after that near Bethel.

> There he built an altar to the LORD and called on the name of the LORD. (Genesis 12:8b NIV)

An altar built to God shows honor and worship to Him as your God. People built altars in the Bible as a normal part of life and a reverent way to worship God. In the same way, we are told to offer ourselves to God through our service to God in special things and in our everyday life.

> I beseech you therefore, brethren, by the mercies of God, that you present your bodies a living sacrifice, holy, acceptable to God, *which is* your reasonable service. (Romans 12:1 NKJV)

> Therefore I urge you, brothers and sisters, by the mercies of God, to present your bodies [dedicating all of yourselves, set apart] as a living sacrifice, holy and well-pleasing to God, *which is* your rational (logical, intelligent) act of worship. (Romans 12:1 AMP)

Abraham worshipped God at the altars that he built. We worship God, but not at an altar of stones. Jesus sacrificed Himself and brought His blood to God as an act of worship, one time for everyone. We go to the altar with our "reasonable service" – our "rational, logical, intelligent act of worship." We do this when we allow God to lead us by His Holy Spirit and as we serve God with our lives.

Jesus told the disciples that He would make them fishers of men. These are people who find and bring people to God. (Matthew 4:19 NKJV) He told Peter to "feed My lambs and My sheep." (John 21 NKJV) These are examples of a sacrifice to God that fulfills Romans 12:1, where he asks for your reasonable service.

God wants an active and constant relationship with you. We already know that He will not "trash us" or abandon us to the world. He actually holds us in His hand.

> So do not fear, for I am with you; do not be dismayed, for I am your God. I will strengthen you and help you; I will uphold you with my righteous right hand. (Isaiah 41:10 NIV)

> For I am the LORD your God who takes hold of your right hand and says to you, Do not fear; I will help you. (Isaiah 41:13 NIV)

This is a great thing knowing that God cares personally for me. He starts the relationship and actively manages it with us. We are involved with God. I cooperate and am actively involved because I am thankful to Him and love Him. This is what Abraham did and it is how believers live a healthy relationship with God.

Abraham understood that God's love and concern for him was a precious thing. While other people were consumed by things of the world and worshipped false gods, Abraham pursed a relationship of obedience and worship. Abraham believed God by exercising faith that He existed and understood that He would bless and keep Him.

Believers today need the same type of relationship with God. A relationship of worship, obedience and faith that responds "YES!" to God. This shows our love to Him. An older song said "what the world needs now is love sweet love, it's the only thing that there's just too little of." This world already has real love because God is love. What the people of this world really need is to receive and live in a relationship with God. In this, believers will be loving God and loving people. This fulfills God's wishes - His perfect will for the world.

This wonderful truth that God is love is clearly seen in John 3:16-17, a verse that many believers know by heart. God loved the world and gave Jesus so we could live and not die. God did not send Jesus to condemn us to death, but rather that we would have eternal life through Him – live forever with God.

In a relationship with God, He is not an acquaintance – someone we know slightly but are not close to. A relationship with God is closer than our family or friends.

> The man of *too many* friends [chosen indiscriminately] will be broken in pieces *and* come to ruin, But there is a [true, loving] friend who [is reliable and] sticks closer than a brother. (Proverbs 18:24 AMP)

My mother use to tell us, "Choose your friends wisely." Believers should choose their friends using wisdom. Do not befriend people who are going to drag you down spiritually without God's direction to do so. The second half of this proverb tells us about a friend who sticks closer than a brother. This is a perfect picture of our Lord Jesus. He is telling us, "I am not your acquaintance or distant cousin. I am very close friend, closer than your immediate family." He said we are not servants or slaves, but that we have the relationship of all being family members.

> I do not call you servants any longer, for the servant does not know what his master is doing; but I have called you [My] friends, because I have revealed to you everything that I have heard from My Father. (John 15:15 AMP)

Our close friend Jesus Christ established a relationship with us. A deep, eternal relationship where are brought into His family. We are family with Jesus, our heavenly Father, the Holy Spirit and all of the saints who are in heaven and all the saints here on the earth. Thank God for His family and that we are made a part of His family. We are active and eternal family members.

Maybe you have a family where the bonds were definitely close with one another – birthdays, holidays, weddings, funerals, etc. My family always celebrated holidays with enthusiasm. We ate together, played together and sang together. We are a close family. This is how believers are with God. Our relationship with God is greater than that of a close family, an unbreakable relationship.

In the Gospels, Jesus called twelve fellows to follow Him – the twelve disciples. He valued a relationship with them and during the time while Jesus was on earth, they learned to value a relationship with Him. All except Judas, who betrayed Him and sold Him to His cruel death.

In our close relationship as a friend, we talk to God (prayer) one-on-one and face-to-face. We read what He says in His Word (our Bible). We fellowship with the other friends of God (other believers) and work together with them to spread His Kingdom.

> You are my friends if you do what I command. (John 15:14 NIV)

> Therefore, go and make disciples of all nations, baptizing them in the name of the Father and of the Son and of the Holy Spirit, and teaching them to obey everything I have commanded you. And surely, I am with you always, to the very end of the age. (Matthew 28:19-20 NIV)

Friends cooperate and work together. We work together with God and believe what He says. We are led by the Holy Spirit and fellowship with other believers. Abraham was a friend of God because he trusted God.

> And the scripture was fulfilled that says, "Abraham believed God, and it was credited to him as righteousness," and he was called God's friend. (James 2:23 NIV)

Abraham's trust was so complete that he packed up his family to follow where God would lead him, not knowing his final destination. God called Abraham, he answered, and he obeyed. This is what we do. We are believers in Christ – we answer and obey. This is the relationship we have with God. He is our friend.

Jesus taught us to talk to our heavenly Father as we talk to our family. (Matthew 6:9) In our relationship with God, we actually talk with our friend.

> Jesus answered, "I am the way and the truth and the life. No one comes to the Father except through me. If you really know me, you

will know my Father as well. From now on, you do know him and have seen him." (John 14:6-7 NIV)

This verse shows the oneness we have through Jesus with our Father. Oneness. People need to lose the attitude that God is distant from us. God is near to us. (Psalm 145:18) Jesus personally brought us to the Father, and He said we know Him and we have seen Him.

> Those who accept my commandments and obey them are the ones who love me. And because they love me, my Father will love them. And I will love them and reveal myself to each of them. (John 14:21 NLT)

We love Jesus because He first loved us. We do what He says in obedience because we love Him. I love Jesus and seek to obey Him. My desire is to please Him and bring Him joy through worship and obedience coming from a sincere and thankful heart.

In marriage ceremonies, we take vows to love and honor each other. What begins as romance, grows and buds into a wedding and a marriage.

The Church of Jesus Christ is the bride of Christ.

> Husbands, love your wives, as Christ loved the church and gave himself up for her, that he might sanctify her, having cleansed her by the washing of water with the word, so that he might present the church to himself in

> splendor, without spot or wrinkle or any such thing, that she might be holy and without blemish. (Ephesians 5:25-27 ESV)
>
> Let us rejoice and exult and give him the glory, for the marriage of the Lamb has come, and his Bride has made herself ready; it was granted her to clothe herself with fine linen, bright and pure" - for the fine linen is the righteous deeds of the saints. And the angel said to me, "Write this: Blessed are those who are invited to the marriage supper of the Lamb." And he said to me, "These are the true words of God." (Revelation 19:7-9 ESV)

Men are instructed in Ephesians to have a great love for our wives, in the same way that Christ loves His bride, the Church. This lasting relationship is one of a close knowledge of each other. Jesus will find His bride dressed in white linen and pure. He so desires to permanently be with us. The bride will be reunited with Christ (Revelation 19) and we will be together with Him forever.

The author, Oswald Chambers once wrote, "The most important aspect of Christianity is not the work we do, but the relationship we maintain [with God] and the surrounding influence and qualities produced by that relationship. That is all God asks us to give our attention to, and it is the one thing that is continually under attack." (Used with permission)

Our relationship with God is the most important thing in our lives. The devil hates this relationship because he hates God. The devil is powerless to stop our relationship with God.

> The thief comes only to steal and kill and destroy; I have come that they may have life, and have it to the full. (John 10:10 NIV)

The thief is the devil and he wants to steal, kill and destroy God's life in us and our relationship with Him. Jesus has defeated the devil and has made him powerless unless we yield to his lies and deception.

We see this same deception from the devil when he was tempting Jesus in the wilderness. He tried to get Jesus to deny God His Father in the same way we are tempted to deny God and stop trusting Him. It's all a lie and a deception.

In contrast to the lies and deception, God had given believers a full and abundant life. He brings a relationship to believers, provides all of our needs and we are redeemed for eternity. We have eternal life – it starts now on earth and extends forever.

Society tells us to "think BIG!" I believe in thinking BIG in God. We are people that have an active relationship with God. We talk with Him and listen to Him. We obey what He says. We dream BIG dreams for God, dreams that He gives us. Dreams that are the will of God. Dreams that He can bless as we obey Him. A believer relies upon that relationship to help him think "God thoughts" – revelations, dreams, ideas and concepts from God that bring Him glory and honor. We hear what He says because we are in constant contact with Him.

A relationship with God is the only reason we live. This relationship with God is compared with the vine and the branch parable told in John 15. Jesus talked about something that they would be familiar with – grapevines. Jesus told them about the true vine.

> I am the true grapevine, and my Father is the gardener. Remain in me, and I will remain in you. For a branch cannot produce fruit if it is severed from the vine, and you cannot be fruitful unless you remain in me. (John 15:1,4 NLT)

We see that there is a relationship between every believer, the Father and Jesus Christ. Jesus is the *true* vine. *True* is the opposite of counterfeit, pretend, imperfect, defective and uncertain. This means that Jesus is the "real deal" – He is genuine, perfect, certain and guaranteed. Jesus is what He says He is. He does not lie, deceive or cheat people because He cannot lie – He is the Truth.

We *abide* in Him. (NKJV) This means that we settle down and remain and *abide* in the Vine for our entire life. Jesus, the genuine Vine is a place that we survive and live abundantly. Our relationship with God is permanent.

Fruitfulness of the believer for God is the expectation of every believer. We live in Him; we receive our nourishment and life from Him. Because we love Him, we take direction from Him. As with the grapevine, the outcome of this relationship with the Vine is producing fruit.

This relationship with God brings the believer to love and cherish God by holding Him dear above everyone else and everything else. We love God because He first loved us. (1 John 4:19) We love God because of the caring relationship we have with Him. This love in the relationship is the fruit which is the result of our relationship.

The fruit that grows when we abide in the Vine is shown in our appreciation of our relationship with God. Believers tell others the good news by spreading the Gospel. Believers help people because the love of God is the motivating factor. We show God's love in our relationships with family, friends and strangers. All of this is a result of the relationship of abiding in the true Vine.

"The Lord is my shepherd; I shall not want." (Psalm 23:1 NKJV) Shepherds provide all of the needs of the sheep and have a relationship of care and loyalty with their sheep. Sheep lack nothing and believers lack nothing. Jesus, the Good Shepherd cares for us because He loves us. We could say He takes us to pasture to eat and brings us to water to drink.

> I am the good shepherd; I know my sheep and my sheep know me — just as the Father knows me and I know the Father — and I lay down my life for the sheep. (John 10:14-15 NIV)

Jesus is vigilant and protects us. He laid down His life for the sheep when He gave His life at the cross to redeem us back to God.

God takes care of the believers. He is our companion and our special friend. He sticks closer to us than our dearest family member.

> There are "friends" who destroy each other, but a real friend sticks closer than a brother. (Proverbs 18:24 NLT)

People are hurt and even betrayed by "friends" in the same way that Judas betrayed Jesus. Jesus is our friend and we are eternally in His family. We are believers and we are made a permanent family member - no divorces, no banishment and no giving up on us. "You are out of the family" is something we will never hear. Our membership in the family is permanent and eternal. He guarantees it.

> for He has said, "I will never [under any circumstances] desert you [nor give you up nor leave you without support, nor will I in any degree leave you helpless], nor will I forsake *or* relax My hold on you [assuredly not]! (Hebrews 13:5 AMP)

We seek the Kingdom of God first (Matthew 6:33) – ahead of everything and with a deep sense of loyalty. All believers are important individuals in the Kingdom – citizens and family of the King.

> Who is this King of glory? The Lord of hosts, he is the King of glory. *Selah.* (Psalm 24:10 KJV).

Christians talk about a "personal relationship" with Jesus, to the point of it almost being considered a cliche or a slogan. The truth is that our relationship with Jesus is personal. He knows us personally and He would have died for <u>every</u> believer if they were the only one. His love for us is personal and we relate to Him personally. These are one-on-one connections with God, again, as if we were the only one on earth that needed Him. We are connected by blood with Jesus as family members are connected by blood. Jesus was close to His disciples in spite of all of their imperfections. He had a personal relationship with them that was very apparent in the Gospels.

This relationship begins with faith. We receive Jesus as our personal Savior when we sincerely call to Him and honor Him as Lord. We sincerely believe that after He died, God definitely raised Him from the dead. This is how we become a member of God's family and enter that relationship with God. (Romans 10:9-10 paraphrase) The believer goes on and grows in their relationship with God. It is a "forever" relationship and deeply personal between the believer and God.

I am my beloved's, and my beloved is mine.
(Song of Solomon 6:3a NKJV)

Today is your day of a new and lasting relationship with God that will grow and increase.

Chapter Questions

1. What is a relationship?

2. What is a relationship with God?

3. Why should a believer not love money?

4. Believers have a permanent relationship with God. How is this possible?

5. The disciples were "fishers of men." Today, how are believers fishers of men?

6. Briefly describe your friendship with Jesus. How is Jesus your friend?

7. On page 5, we read about Abraham. How did he demonstrate his faith in God?

8. How is loving a wife like loving Christ? How is loving a wife different?

9. Write one sentence and tell one thing about your relationship with God.

10. Why is <u>your</u> relationship with God important?

Chapter 3

Our High Priest

We are told to consider Jesus, our Apostle and High Priest.

> Therefore, holy brethren, partakers of the heavenly calling, consider the Apostle and High Priest of our confession, Christ Jesus, who was faithful to Him who appointed Him, as Moses also *was faithful* in all His house. (Hebrews 3:1-2 NKJV)

> And so, dear brothers and sisters who belong to God and are partners with those called to heaven, think carefully about this Jesus whom we declare to be God's messenger and High Priest. For he was faithful to God, who appointed him, just as Moses served faithfully when he was entrusted with God's entire house. (Hebrews 3:1-2 NLT)

When we *consider* someone, we work hard to gain understanding and attentively focus our mind upon them. Jesus is God's messenger to us and God's High Priest for us. He remained faithful to God and fully accomplished His mission. Jesus was faithful and obedient because He loved God and He loved us. He knew His faithfulness and obedience would bear fruit with God that would benefit everyone who believed.

When we consider Jesus, we think about all that He has done for us. We consider His faithfulness to God. Jesus obeyed God in spite of all of the extreme suffering that He would experience.

When we look at Moses, we read about his faithfulness to God. He was faithful to bring the children of Israel out of Egypt and bring the Law of God to the people. When God gave the Law to Israel through Moses, He appointed Aaron to be High Priest. Aaron's responsibility was to go to God and present the sacrifice for the sins of the people.

In the relationship that Israel had with God, they were represented by the earthly High Priest. This High Priest brought sacrifices to God for Israel's sins. We consider that our High Priest Jesus was sent by God to represent us before God. Our High Priest went to God for us as individuals and for us as His people the Church. After the sacrifice when He was crucified, resurrected and brought His blood sacrifice to God, He justified us. The sacrifice of His perfect blood was totally effective and better than the blood of bulls and goats.

Man rebelled against God and the horrible sin that was committed broke the relationship that man had with God. It brought separation from God. The perfect sacrifice of Jesus restored our relationship with God.

Our High Priest was obedient and went to God for us. Jesus brought us back to God.

> God made him who had no sin to be sin for us, so that in him we might become the righteousness of God. (2 Corinthians 5:21 NIV)

> God put the wrong on him who never did anything wrong, so we could be put right with God. (2 Corinthians 5:21 MSG)

Our restored relationship that was by Christ was one of righteousness. Believers are actually made totally righteous by God because of what Christ did. Christ was made sin and we were made righteous. Thank God for Jesus, our eternal High Priest. (Hebrew 6:20)

Aaron the High Priest was human and eventually die. Melchizedek (Genesis 14:18-20) the High Priest to the Most High God was different – he had no beginning and no end.

> This Melchizedek was king of Salem and priest of God Most High. He met Abraham returning from the defeat of the kings and blessed him, and Abraham gave him a tenth of everything. First, the name Melchizedek means "king of righteousness"; then also, "king of Salem" means "king of peace." Without father or mother, without genealogy, without beginning of days or end of life, resembling the Son of God, he remains a priest forever. (Hebrews 7:1-3 NIV)

Melchizedek was the King of Salem (Salem means *peace*) and the King of Righteousness (Melchizedek means *righteousness*). *Peace* is harmony between individuals. In this case, it is harmony between God and Melchizedek. *Righteousness* is the state of someone who is acceptable to God. Faith mixed with the perfect sacrifice of Jesus washed the wicked sin from people. Jesus, our High Priest was an eternal High Priest that was able to bring a better sacrifice than the men who were the Levitical priesthood. With His sacrifice Jesus washed sin completely away.

> If perfection could have been attained through the Levitical priesthood — and indeed the law given to the people established that priesthood — why was there still need for another priest to come, one in the order of Melchizedek, not in the order of Aaron? (Hebrews 7:11 NIV)

Jesus had to come to bring a better sacrifice than the sacrifices the Levites brought. Jesus brought a sacrifice that was better because it was perfect. God offered Jesus as the perfect sinless sacrifice to wash away sin and bring righteousness to everyone. We have eternal life and a strong relationship with God because of His sacrifice.

Jesus is the eternal High Priest who can bring true peace and righteousness to people. This peace brings new life and a life of security and satisfaction. No longer do we have worry and fret over the issues of life. We can now live a life of trusting God. The righteousness that Christ our eternal High Priest brings changes us from sin and death and brings us into a beautiful living relationship with God.

> Now there have been many of those priests, since death prevented them from continuing in office; but because Jesus lives forever, he has a permanent priesthood. (Hebrews 7:23-24 NIV)

When the High Priest on earth died, a new High Priest would be appointed. Christ is eternal and therefore our permanent High Priest. He is permanently seated at God's right hand interceding to God for us. He will always be there for each of us because He loves us.

> Such a high priest [Jesus] truly meets our need — one who is holy, blameless, pure, set apart from sinners, exalted above the heavens. Unlike the other high priests, he does not need to offer sacrifices day after day, first for his own sins, and then for the sins of the people. He sacrificed for their sins once for all when he offered himself. (Hebrews 7:26-27 NIV)

Our High Priest is perfect and brought the perfect sacrifice of His blood. He went to God with His sacrifice one time and does not need to go back to God again every time someone sins. His sacrifice was "once for all."

The sacrifices that were made by the Levitical priesthood could not bring a solution that would fix the problem of sin. The sacrifices of the priesthood were imperfect and were made for imperfect people. These sacrifices would not permanently forgive sin, but were temporary and imperfect. But because our High Priest brought a perfect sacrifice, <u>all</u> of the sins of man were finally forgiven.

People everywhere can trust what Jesus did. Following Jesus is not a western or an American thing. His ministry brought an eternal and permanent relationship with God for all the people of the world. Believers are forgiven, righteous and can now go to God. We were previously away from God and faced with the impossibility of never being one with God. We are now close to God and we are in Christ.

> But now in Christ Jesus you who once were far away have been brought near by the blood of Christ. (Ephesians 2:13 NIV)

Because Jesus is a High Priest, it was His duty to bring a sacrifice to God for the people. His perfect sacrifice was the exact solution to fix the problem of sin and bring man total forgiveness.

The specific type of sacrifice for a certain celebration or sin is listed in the Law. A good example of bringing a sacrifice in obedience to the Law is seen when Mary and Joseph brought Jesus to the Temple in Jerusalem.

> When the time came for the purification rites required by the Law of Moses, Joseph and Mary took him to Jerusalem to present him to

> the Lord (as it is written in the Law of the Lord, "Every firstborn male is to be consecrated to the Lord"), and to offer a sacrifice in keeping with what is said in the Law of the Lord: "a pair of doves or two young pigeons. (Luke 2:22-24 NIV)
>
> The law of the Lord says, "If a woman's first child is a boy, he must be dedicated to the LORD." (Luke 2:23 NLT)

The requirement for the ceremony of consecration to the Lord is the sacrifice of doves and pigeons. (Exodus 13:2, Leviticus 12:8)

Joseph and Mary's sacrifice was given to obey the Lord. It provided a way for the people to sacrifice with a thankful heart. Bringing a sacrifice to God is an act of faith - "Lord, I know You bless Your people. I am bringing this to you to bless and worship You." The sacrifice acknowledges that He is our God and we choose to obey Him. It's not the doves or the pigeons, a lamb or a goat, it's the obedience to God when bringing the sacrifice to Him.

> But Samuel replied, "What is more pleasing to the LORD: your burnt offerings and sacrifices or your obedience to his voice? Listen! Obedience is better than sacrifice, and submission is better than offering the fat of rams. (1 Samuel 15:22 NLT)

A thankful and obedient heart desires to give sacrifices to the Lord. This act of sacrificial giving to God is done by faith to the God we love and obey.

We are told that "faith without works is dead." (James 2:26b NIV) This scripture is used to justify much of the charitable works that are normal for a church – feeding the homeless, food banks, building churches in poor nations, digging wells in an African village and so on. This is an accurate application of this principle, but *works* also means *actions that correspond with what we believe.* In James, the idea of *works* is used to describe Abraham's faith and the corresponding actions that he did to tangibly demonstrate his faith.

> Don't you remember that our ancestor Abraham was shown to be right with God by his actions when he offered his son Isaac on the altar? You see, his faith and his actions worked together. His actions made his faith complete. And so it happened just as the Scriptures say: "Abraham believed God, and God counted him as righteous because of his faith." He was even called the friend of God. So you see, we are shown to be right with God by what we do, not by faith alone. (James 21-24 NLT)

Abraham's faith and his actions worked together to confirm that he was serious with God. He heard from God, packed up and left his home. He followed God in the relationship that God brought.

Mary and Joseph confirmed their faith in God time after time. She became pregnant supernaturally by the Holy Spirit and carried the Messiah to birth. Joseph kept Mary and took her as his wife in spite of the fact that she was pregnant and all of the ridicule they would endure. They brought Jesus to the Temple for consecration, their faith in God was very apparent. All of their actions corresponded with their faith. Their faith in God was shown to be genuine because they did what God told them to do. This simple action answers the question, "How do I prove that I have faith in God within me?" Obedience demonstrates our faith and an active relationship with God.

As with the consecration of Jesus in the Temple, our son was dedicated to the Lord at church. We promised to raise our son as a Christian and teach him to follow the Lord. The component that is different under the Law is the bringing of a physical sacrifice to the Lord. Both were heartfelt acts of faith and obedience to God.

When our High Priest brought the sacrifice offering for us, it was unique because He was the offering. The sacrifice of His body and His blood was brought to God.

> you were redeemed from the empty way of life... with the precious blood of Christ, a lamb without blemish or defect. (1 Peter 1:18-19 NIV)

> By that will we have been sanctified through the offering of the body of Jesus Christ once *for all*. (Hebrews 10:10 NKJV)

> The very next day John saw Jesus coming toward him and yelled out, "Here he is, God's Passover Lamb! He forgives the sins of the world!" (John 1:29 MSG)

The only sacrifice that would be accepted by God was offered – Jesus the perfect Lamb of God. We are sanctified (separated from unholy things and dedicated to God) and redeemed (bought back from the adversary and eternal death) by the sacrifice of His blood.

As our High Priest, the ministry of Jesus and His sacrifice was superior.

> But now Jesus, our High Priest, has been given a ministry that is far superior to the old priesthood, for he is the one who mediates for us a far better covenant with God, based on better promises. If the first covenant had been faultless, there would have been no need for a second covenant to replace it. (Hebrews 8:6-7 NLT)

The first covenant brought a relationship between God and man. But man was unable to be forgiven and made righteous in Christ without the death and resurrection of Jesus. He brought new covenant that was backed up by superior promises. In the new covenant man can be redeemed, justified, and made one with God.

The first covenant was only a shadow of the good things that would come in the second covenant. There was a separation between God and man. This separation was cancelled and removed by God when <u>our</u> High Priest brought the perfect sacrifice and earned our redemption. This is why we can have a relationship with God. We are now made righteous in Christ and one with God.

In the first covenant (Old Testament), the priests brought the people's sacrifices to God and made intercession for them. Mary and Joseph brought Jesus and their sacrifice to the priest to consecrate their son to God. It was the duty of the priest to intercede with God and bring their sacrifice to God. The priest went to God for them under the first covenant.

In the second covenant, our High Priest brought the sacrifice of His blood and satisfied the price for the sin of mankind. We were reunited with God and given eternal life when we received Jesus. He still makes intercession with God for people when they come to Him.

> Therefore, he is able, once and forever, to save those who come to God through him. He lives forever to intercede with God on their behalf. (Hebrews 7:25 NLT)

People come to Him when they see the need for God in their life. Jesus brought His blood and intercedes with God for their salvation. Jesus went directly to the Father when He presented His sacrifice one time for everyone. God accepted His blood as the perfect offering which meant that man's sin was paid for and they could now be redeemed. This is the intercession Christ made for people. We have a better hope in Christ than the people did under the Law. In Christ we have a living High Priest and an eternal relationship with our God who dearly loves us.

God is merciful to us. He shows His faithful love though His mercy. His mercy will always be there – it endures forever. He loved us before we were born and knew He would send Jesus for us. He loves us now and for all eternity.

> So then, since we have a great High Priest who has entered heaven, Jesus the Son of God, let us hold firmly to what we believe. This High Priest of ours understands our weaknesses, for he faced all of the same testings we do, yet he did not sin. So let us come boldly to the throne of our gracious God. There we will receive his mercy, and we will find grace to help us when we need it most. (Hebrews 4:14-16 NLT)

In the Old Testament, the earthly High Priest and the priesthood had the same human weaknesses we have. Jesus lived as a human on earth and was subject to the same weaknesses. In spite of this, He never sinned. Therefore, He understands our weaknesses about the places where we stumble and fall. He brings us to God and we receive His mercy and His favor when we need it. Thank God that His mercy endures forever.

How should we relate to God? We relate to Him in our one-to-one relationship. He is our Father and we are His children. Jesus spent time a lot of time talking with His Father – worshipping and loving Him, talking about the needs of people and receiving His instruction.

God is also our Father and we relate to Him with the same closeness that Jesus did and with a greater closeness than many people have with their earthly family. If your relationship with your family was not good, then establish a strong closeness with your heavenly Father, with Jesus and the Holy Spirit – it's a "24/7 thing." The importance of becoming a part of a church is shown in the relationships we establish as we worship God together and develop friendships within the family of God.

Through His loyalty and obedience to God, Jesus our High Priest shows us the type of relationship we should have with God. He approached His heavenly Father with faith and confidence knowing that God was with Him. Jesus understood that God was absolutely trustworthy. He will not and cannot lie because He is the Truth.

> But blessed is the one who trusts in
> the LORD, whose confidence is in him.
> (Jeremiah 17:7 NIV)

> For the Scriptures tell us, "Abraham believed
> God, and God counted him as righteous
> because of his faith." (Romans 4:3 NLT)

> God is not human, that he should lie, not a
> human being, that he should change his mind.
> Does he speak and then not act? Does he
> promise and not fulfill? (Numbers 23:19 NIV)

> The entirety of Your word *is* truth, And every
> one of Your righteous judgements endures
> forever. (Psalms 119:160 NKJV)

Jesus understood that He had to <u>maintain</u> a relationship with God so He could walk closely with Him. To walk with God, we must have an active relationship with God. We talk to Him, we read His Word (the Bible) and we work together and spend time with His saints (fellowship).

> What if the LORD had not been on our side? Let
> all Israel repeat: What if the LORD had not been
> on our side when people attacked us?
> Praise the LORD, who did not let their teeth tear
> us apart! We escaped like a bird from a
> hunter's trap. The trap is broken, and we are
> free! Our help is from the LORD, who made
> heaven and earth. (Psalm 124.1-2, 6-8 NLT)

Our very life is tied up in our relationship with Him. The song *In the Garden* explains this relationship very well and shows our closeness to Him.

> I come to the garden alone
> While the dew is still on the roses
> And the voice I hear falling on my ear
> The Son of God discloses
>
> And He walks with me
> And He talks with me
> And He tells me I am his own
> And the joy we share as we tarry there
> None other has ever known
>
> (*In the Garden*, C. Austin Miles / Robert Hebble, Copyright: *Public Domain*)

In the song, I am especially captivated by the words "And He walks with me and He talks with me..." I want to spend time with God in this way. I want my relationship with Him to be close, glorious and an integral part of my life. When I am with Him, I want to listen to Him and talk to Him. He is my friend and I love Him.

In the last two lines of the song, the lyrics mention *the joy we share as we tarry there*. *Tarrying* is a word that means to stay longer than expected. When we are with Jesus, we don't want to leave. Our relationship with Jesus is a precious thing that we spend time maintaining. We "keep it real" with honesty, heartfelt sharing and all of the things we do to respect the importance of our relationship with God. What a wonderful thing to remain in a relationship with our Lord!

In the song we saw, "we walk with Him and we talk with Him and He tells me I am His own." Today, Jesus is not here physically. But the Holy Spirit teaches and helps every believer. I will be able to learn and fellowship with God as I walk according to the leading of the Holy Spirit.

> But when the Father sends the Advocate as my representative - that is, the Holy Spirit - he will teach you everything and will remind you of everything I have told you. (John 14:26 NLT)

In the Garden was inspired by John 20:1-18. This is the author's story of the meeting between Jesus and Mary Magdalene soon after his resurrection. Jesus and Mary Magdalene had a teacher/student relationship, because Jesus was her rabbi (teacher). Believers have a relationship with God – Jesus is our rabbi (teacher). The Holy Spirit lives inside of believers and they are guided and taught by Him.

Jesus may not be here physically, but God is with us and in us by the Holy Spirit. Believers have a relationship with Him that is sure, steady and real. As we listen to the Holy Spirit, we are guided into all truth and receive from Him.

The Levitical High Priest had a real but legal-based relationship with God because they lived under the Law. The High Priest loved God and worshipped God, but there was a "wall" of sin that separated people from God. This sin is the same separation that is experienced today between the unsaved people of the world and God. Believers have a closeness and oneness with God with no separation from Him.

However, there is relief from sin in Christ Jesus. Believers are totally delivered and experience freedom that can only come because of Jesus. Everyone has sinned and they all fall short of God's holy standards, but Jesus liberated mankind us from sin through His death burial and resurrection.

> Yet God, in his grace, [He] freely makes us right in his sight. (Romans 3:24 NLT)

> We are made right with God by placing our faith in Jesus Christ. And this is true for everyone who believes, no matter who we are. (Romans 3:22 NLT)

This is how personal relationship with God through Jesus Christ works. We place our faith in Jesus Christ. It is more than having a mental agreement with the idea that Jesus existed years ago and "I need to go to church." It is more than reading your Bible. It is accepting Jesus as your Lord and Savior and saying that God raised Jesus from the dead.

In all of this, we acknowledge Jesus as the High Priest and our representative before God. We go to God through Christ. We develop our relationship with God through Christ and we live our life before and in God through Christ.

Thank God for sending Jesus our High Priest for each of us. Thank God that He cares for us and actively helps us on a one-to-one basis. He keeps His relationship with us and loves us. Thank God.

Chapter Questions

1. Identify at least one way that a believer *considers* Jesus. (Hebrews 3)

2. Describe how <u>you</u> *consider* Jesus. What things do you do in your life to make this a success?

3. Moses was faithful to God. What was something he did to show his faithfulness to God?

4. What happened to the relationship between God and man when Adam and Eve sinned against God?

5. What are one or more <u>differences</u> between the High Priest that was on earth and Jesus the High Priest of all believers?

6. How were the High Priest that was on earth and Jesus the High Priest of all believers similar?

7. Why is Jesus a *better* High Priest? (Remember, it's not a *good* or *bad*, but why was He a *better* High Priest?)

8. Who brought the New Covenant between God and man? Why is the New Covenant a *better* covenant?

9. God loves us dearly. What is one way that <u>you</u> have experienced God's love in your life?

10. What did Jesus do to maintain a close relationship with God? What should a believer do to also maintain a close relationship with God?

Chapter 4

Enter God's Rest

God has a wonderful rest prepared for His people. He loves the people of God and wants them to enter His rest. Our righteous relationship with God through Christ brings us into that rest.

> So there is a special rest still waiting for the people of God. For all who have entered into God's rest have rested from their labors, just as God did after creating the world. So let us do our best to enter that rest. But if we disobey God, as the people of Israel did, we will fall. (Hebrews 4:9-11 NLT)

> The promise of "arrival" and "rest" is still there for God's people. God himself is at rest. And at the end of the journey, we'll surely rest with God. So, let's keep at it and eventually arrive at the place of rest, not drop out through some sort of disobedience. (Hebrews 4:9-11 MSG)

The beginning of Psalm 95 shows the joy of loving God.

> Come, let us sing for joy to the LORD; let us shout aloud to the Rock of our salvation. Let us come before him with thanksgiving and extol him with music and song. (Psalm 95:1-2 NIV)

The psalmist encourages them to sing to the Lord and appreciate Him. The reader is told to shout with joy, kneel before Him and come to Him thankfully! He personally holds each of us in His hands and we are the tender flock He cares for. The personal care that God has for us is plenty to get excited about.

The reader is encouraged to hear Him and warned to obey Him.

> If only you would listen to his [God's] voice today! (Psalm 95:7b NLT)

The Psalm talks about the rebellion and hard-heartedness of the people and God says

> For forty years I was angry with them, and I said, 'They are a people whose hearts turn away from me. They refuse to do what I tell them.' So, in my anger I took an oath: 'They will never enter my place of rest.'" (Psalm 95:10-11 NLT)

The rebelliousness of Israel began soon after they left Egypt. Over the years, they would serve other gods and kill the prophets that God sent to warn and correct them. They were eventually captured and exiled to Syria and Babylon.

But, what about the people who had faith in God and had their faith counted as righteousness?

> Was not our father Abraham considered righteous for what he did when he offered his son Isaac on the altar? (James 2:22 NIV)

> In the same way, was not even Rahab the prostitute considered righteous for what she did when she gave lodging to the spies and sent them off in a different direction? (James 2:25 NIV)

These were righteous people that entered into His rest through their life of faith. Their faith in God was counted as righteousness before God. How did Abraham and Rahab enter into His righteousness and His rest? Were these people special or is this rest available to believers now? No. They were righteous because of their faith in Him. We become righteous when we have faith in Him.

God pays attention to what you say to Him.

> I love the LORD, for he heard my voice; he heard my cry for mercy. Because He has inclined His ear to me, Therefore I will call on Him as long as I live. (Psalm 116:1 AMP)

Believers are made righteous and talk to God as a normal part of life. Our righteous relationship with Him brings us into His rest. In the Psalm, we see some people who worshipped and obeyed God. We also saw people who rebelled against God because they wanted to be independent of God – they considered themselves "self-made" and did not want God interfering in their lives. God desires for us to rest in Him. Believers' relationship with Him brings His rest. Righteousness in Christ is the lifestyle we desire and follow.

> Understand, therefore, that the LORD your God is indeed God. He is the faithful God who keeps his covenant for a thousand generations and lavishes his unfailing love on those who love him and obey his commands. (Deuteronomy 7:9 NLT)

His unfailing love is lavished upon us and comes when we are made righteous through His salvation. We do this by faith. Believers trust, believe and follow Him and enter into His rest.

The choice remains – enter His rest or do not enter His rest.

> Now we who have believed enter that rest, just as God has said, "So I declared on oath in my anger, 'They shall never enter my rest.'" (Hebrews 4:3 NIV)

> Therefore, since it still remains for some to enter that rest, and since those who formerly had the good news proclaimed to them did not go in because of their disobedience, (Hebrews 4:6 NIV)

This is a clear set of choices that God Himself offers to everyone – all people everywhere.

The word *rest* (as in relax) in this context literally means to lay down and is used in Acts.

> "However, the Most High does not live in houses made by human hands. As the prophet says: "'Heaven is my throne, and the earth is my footstool. What kind of house will you build for me? says the Lord. Or where will my resting place be? Has not my hand made all these things?' (Acts 7:48-50 NIV)

God is asking, "even if I lived in a house, what kind of house would you build for Me?" The point being made here is "I don't need a house to dwell in or a bed to rest in."

Our rest from God is not taking a nap on the couch (though that would be nice!). Our rest is an attitude that tells God that you trust Him. We trust Him and live a life of faith and trust just like Abraham. We will follow God wherever He leads us. This is a life of faith and the rest of God.

I coached middle school track and my athletes worked hard to be ready for their events. They prepared by using a training regimen. Some of the athletes trained for field events like shot put, some for the longer distances like the mile and others the shorter sprints and hurdles. All of the athletes worked hard. They endured the pain and exhaustion that an athlete experiences.

Hebrews tells us to get ready for the "race" that God has given each of us.

> Therefore, since we are surrounded by such a huge crowd of witnesses to the life of faith, let us strip off every weight that slows us down, especially the sin that so easily trips us up. And let us run with endurance the race God has set before us. (Hebrews 12:1 NLT)

This scripture concerns preparing to serve God to successfully complete God's assignment and fulfill His expectations for each of us. What's your race? Raising a family? Taking Bible school courses? Serving as a Sunday School teacher? Working hard to provide for your family? All of these involve trusting God along with an attitude of endurance. We trust God and are diligent to do what He assigns.

In the same ways that athletes get tired, those serving God become physically tired, as well as emotionally spent. Athletes know that proper nutrition and getting enough rest are the answers to fatigue. We have all heard of the special diets that elite athletes stick to. Believers must do the same – proper nutrition of feeding off the Word of God (reading your Bible), spending time in prayer (talking to God) and fellowship with other believers. This is the "special diet" that the believer must have. The family of God's children provides support and adds energy to the believer. Trusting God in faith brings the rest we need. All of these together will equip the believer to be ready for whatever God calls us to do, just like a pro football player who trains to get ready for the BIG Sunday game!

As both the athlete and believer prepare, Jesus tells us to go to Him.

> Take my yoke upon you. Let me teach you, because I am humble and gentle at heart, and you will find rest for your souls. For my yoke is easy to bear, and the burden I give you is light. (Matthew 11:29-30 NLT)
>
> Take My yoke upon you and learn from Me [following Me as My disciple], for I am gentle and humble in heart, and YOU WILL FIND REST (renewal, blessed quiet) FOR YOUR SOULS. For My yoke is easy [to bear] and My burden is light. (Matthew 11:29-30 AMP)

We go to Jesus in obedience when we serve Him. We join together (yoke) with Him and are not exhausted and "beaten half to death" with hard, burdensome labor. Instead, we are treated with kindness and love by God. This is rest for our souls where we are refreshed in our spirit, soul and body. We know that we have been with God. His yoke is easy – we can follow and obey Him. His burden is light.

Many righteous believers are there to encourage us and cheer us on.

> Therefore, since we are surrounded by such a great cloud of witnesses, let us throw off everything that hinders and the sin that so

easily entangles. And let us run with perseverance the race marked out for us, (Hebrews 12:1 NIV)

Therefore, since we are surrounded by such a huge crowd of witnesses to the life of faith, let us strip off every weight that slows us down, especially the sin that so easily trips us up. And let us run with endurance the race God has set before us. (Hebrews 12:1 NLT)

Do you see what this means—all these pioneers who blazed the way, all these veterans cheering us on? It means we'd better get on with it. Strip down, start running—and never quit! No extra spiritual fat, no parasitic sins. (Hebrews 12:1 MSG)

Believers are surrounded by many saints here on earth and in heaven. We can trust and follow their example as we serve God. The saints encourage us with their words and testimony of following God. Today, even that small simple word of encouragement given to someone can really make the difference in their life.

How do we follow the example of these witnesses? We keep our spiritual eyes on our Savior, Jesus Christ.

> fixing our eyes on Jesus, the pioneer and perfecter of faith. For the joy set before him he endured the cross, scorning its shame, and sat

down at the right hand of the throne of God.
(Hebrews 12:2 NIV)

Jesus endured the hardships and served God without sin. He kept His eyes upon His Father. Believers train and serve God. It is critical to stay in the rest of God. All believers need to rest confidently in God.

> He walked away, about a stone's throw, and knelt down and prayed, "Father, if you are willing, please take this cup of suffering away from me. Yet I want your will to be done, not mine." (Luke 21:41-42 NLT)

Jesus endured horrible torture and death so He could bring us to God. He started our faith and He completed our faith. This brought Him joy. He knew that we would be made righteous in Him and that we could come home to God, being totally forgiven and completely clean. Jesus did all of the work and paid the costly price so that believers could be reunited with God.

David had a close relationship with God. In the psalms he wrote that his relationship with God was strong. David was called by God and anointed by the prophet Samuel to be king of Israel. David was pursued by King Saul, actually hunted like a criminal. This kept David on the run to avoid capture and death. David had to walk in his strong relationship and in the rest of God so He could trust God during all of these challenges.

Three verses in Psalm 23 provide an accurate picture of David actively trusting God.

> Yea, though I walk through the valley of the shadow of death, I will fear no evil: for thou art with me; thy rod and thy staff they comfort me. Thou preparest a table before me in the presence of mine enemies: thou anointest my head with oil; my cup runneth over. Surely goodness and mercy shall follow me all the days of my life: and I will dwell in the house of the LORD forever. (Psalm 23:4-6 KJV)

> Even when I walk through the darkest valley, will not be afraid, for you are close beside me. Your rod and your staff protect and comfort me. You prepare a feast for me in the presence of my enemies. You honor me by anointing my head with oil. My cup overflows with blessings. Surely your goodness and unfailing love will pursue me all the days of my life, and I will live in the house of the LORD forever. (Psalm 23:4-6 NLT)

David rested in God, knowing that God was able and willing to help him. God called David a man after His own heart.

> God testified concerning him: 'I have found David son of Jesse, a man after my own heart; he will do everything I want him to do.' (Acts 13:22b NIV)

David was humble.

> O my people, trust in him at all times. Pour out your heart to him, for God is our refuge. *Interlude* Common people are as worthless as a puff of wind, and the powerful are not what they appear to be. If you weigh them on the scales, together they are lighter than a breath of air. (Psalm 62:8-9 NLT)
>
> God has spoken plainly, and I have heard it many times: Power, O God, belongs to you; unfailing love, O Lord, is yours. (Psalm 62:11-12a NLT)

David was reverent.

> I called on the LORD, who is worthy of praise, and he saved me from my enemies. (Psalm 18:3 NIV)

David loved God.

> I love you, LORD; you are my strength. The LORD is my rock, my fortress, and my savior; my God is my rock, in whom I find protection. He is my shield, the power that saves me, and my place of safety. I called on the LORD, who is worthy of praise, and he saved me from my enemies. (Psalm 18:1-3 NLT)

David was devoted to God.

> You have given me greater joy than those who have abundant harvests of grain and new wine. In peace I will lie down and sleep, for you

> alone, O LORD, will keep me safe. (Psalm 4:7-8 NLT)

David was obedient to God.

> Teach me your decrees, O LORD; I will keep them to the end. Give me understanding and I will obey your instructions; I will put them into practice with all my heart. Make me walk along the path of your commands, for that is where my happiness is found. (Psalm 119:33-35 NLT)

David repented before God.

> For the honor of your name, O LORD, forgive my many, many sins. (Psalm 22:11 NLT)

These are spiritual and character qualities that endeared David to God. David sinned so it was definitely clear that he was not perfect. But as we saw, he deeply loved God and was called a man after God's heart. God showed David grace and mercy. David's relationship and rest in God sustained him throughout his life.

Jesus was questioned by a sincere man who wanted to know how to obtain eternal life. However, we will see that there was a problem in his life.

> Just then a man came up to Jesus and asked, "Teacher, what good thing must I do to get eternal life?" "Why do you ask me about what is good?" Jesus replied. "There is only One who is good. If you want to enter life, keep the

> commandments." "Which ones?" he inquired. Jesus replied, "'You shall not murder, you shall not commit adultery, you shall not steal, you shall not give false testimony, honor your father and mother,' and 'love your neighbor as yourself.'" "All these I have kept," the young man said. "What do I still lack?" Jesus answered, "If you want to be perfect, go, sell your possessions and give to the poor, and you will have treasure in heaven. Then come, follow me." When the young man heard this, he went away sad, because he had great wealth. (Matthew 19:16-22 NIV)

Jesus went on to say that it is difficult for rich people to become a part of the kingdom of heaven.

The man went away very disappointed because he had many possessions and great wealth. The text does not say that he immediately went away and sold his possessions. Instead, it says that he went away very sad. I believe that he wanted to become a follower of Jesus and enter God's kingdom. He trusted God in his life. But I also believe that his possessions were so important to him that he trusted in his possessions and being wealthy more than he trusted God. We could say that his possessions and wealth owned him.

> Hear, O Israel: The LORD our God, the LORD is one. Love the LORD your God with all your heart and with all your soul and with all your strength. (Deuteronomy 6:4-5 NIV)

The man knew these Scriptures. He did not love the Lord with all of his heart. This is a sad thing. In contrast, we see Abraham who trusted God so much that he packed up and followed God everywhere He would lead him. The interesting fact is God did not give Abraham advanced notice about where he was going. Some people call this "blind faith." I see it as Abraham's faith in action and his resting in God.

I believe that the man was afraid of losing his possessions and wealth. Possibly he found his identity or prestige in his wealth. Jesus was essentially telling the man, "Lose your stuff by selling it, use the money to help people and follow Me."

The man wanted to obtain eternal life. The man went to the right person – Jesus Christ. It was common knowledge to sincere people who needed something from God that going to Jesus was the answer. The hard-hearted religious leaders constantly harassed Jesus and replaced God with their manmade beliefs about God. Only the sincere people followed Him. The hard-hearted people rejected Him.

Many desperate people came to Jesus for healing, deliverance and to learn the truth about God. Jesus was their only hope.

The rich man came to Jesus with a purpose. He wanted to know God but a hard heart stopped him. He went away very sad. Believers can learn from this disappointing story. We should live for God with purpose. We should believe God with purpose. We should obey God with purpose and love God with purpose. Having purpose is essential and a valuable lesson to learn concerning our relationship with God. When we have purpose, we do something for a reason. We decide and then we do.

By faith, the man could have sold his possessions to follow Jesus and receive eternal life. The man needed to follow the example of Abraham. The man could have had active faith and obedience to God. This would have been counted as righteousness. The man would have known about "father Abraham" and the value in following his example. We can only hope that the man eventually followed God through Jesus Christ.

The offer to the man was eternal life. The man could not allow himself to accept the offer. He chose his possessions instead of God. This is a tragic end to a story full of hope. He could have changed his life. He could have had a relationship with God and entered into His rest. Instead, he was held by his possessions.

Joseph was a just man – he was justified and righteous before God. He had a relationship with God and had entered God's rest. When Mary became pregnant through a miracle by the Holy Spirit, Joseph was going to quietly break the engagement so as to not embarrass her. God told Joseph in a dream to take Mary as his wife. Obeying this requirement of God took courage on his part and entering the rest of God. There would have been plenty of gossip, and Joseph was probably openly criticized by people because of Mary's pregnancy and his decision to obey God. Joseph fulfilled God's will and received the promise of bringing Jesus into the world.

After Jesus' birth, Joseph, Mary and the child Jesus had to flee Israel and go to Egypt because Herod was out to kill Jesus.

> ...an angel of the Lord appeared to Joseph in a dream. "Get up," he said, "take the child and his mother and escape to Egypt. Stay there until I tell you, for Herod is going to search for the child to kill him." So he got up, took the child and his mother during the night and left for Egypt, where he stayed until the death of Herod. And so was fulfilled what the Lord had said through the prophet: "Out of Egypt I called my son." (Matthew 2:13-15 NIV)

Herod eventually killed all of the young boys. This fulfilled a prophecy of Jeremiah found in Jeremiah 31:15.

> A voice is heard in Ramah, weeping and great mourning, Rachel weeping for her children and refusing to be comforted, because they are no more. (Matthew 2:18 NIV)

Joseph had a relationship with God. He was a righteous man who understood and lived a life of obedience to God. His obedience to God brought the rest of God and protection for him and his family. Having a relationship and resting in God gives you the ability to endure the unexpected, to endure hardship while thanking and praising God for His goodness. Believers can learn from the life of Joseph – rest in God.

Having faith in God through Jesus Christ and receiving Jesus as Lord and Savior is how we make contact with God. Our relationship with God is founded upon the scriptures.

> If you declare with your mouth, "Jesus is Lord," and believe in your heart that God raised him from the dead, you will be saved. For it is with your heart that you believe and are justified, and it is with your mouth that you profess your faith and are saved. (Romans 10:9-10 NIV)

We have assurance from this scripture that we will be brought into His kingdom by faith.

John Piper, a pastor from Minneapolis wrote that, "Normal Christian life is aware of the fearful danger of unbelief, but does not live paralyzed or terrorized by it. It lives by faith." Our relationship with God and our resting in God are normal Christian living. These are not only for ministers or "super" Christians, but for every believer. A relationship with God is normal Christian living – something we should seek and receive from God.

Martin Luther, a German Christian (he lived 1483-1546) was terrorized as a student while he attended university. During a lightning storm, he thought that

God was trying to kill him and demanded that he enter the ministry and served Him. God was not trying to kill him. Later, Luther thought the answer was to constantly suffer hardship for God. Eventually he found that "the just shall live by faith" while reading Romans.

> *For therein is the righteousness of God revealed from faith to faith: as it is written, The just shall live by faith. (Romans 1:17 KJV)*

Luther discovered that we make contact with God through faith in Christ and we become righteous through faith in Christ. There was no more need for extreme suffering for God. He did not need to beg God to accept us. Luther learned that by going to God through Jesus Christ he would receive righteousness, acceptance by God and a relationship with God.

Luther was pursued by the religious leaders who opposed his message. They tried to arrest him and he eventually went into hiding. He was persecuted for believing and practicing what the Bible said. He founded churches that preached justification by faith. His churches eventually became the Lutheran church. Luther found his home in God – a relationship with Him and resting in Him. He found from the Scriptures that He did not have to earn righteousness through good works or harsh self-discipline. He learned that he could receive God's righteousness as a gift from God.

> For the sin of this one man, Adam, caused death to rule over many. But even greater is God's wonderful grace and his gift of righteousness, for all who receive it will live in triumph over sin and death through this one man, Jesus Christ. (Romans 5:17 NLT)

The sacrifice and blood of Jesus eradicated sin and death. Man had earned death because of sin, but received the gift of eternal life through Jesus Christ.

> the free gift of God [that is, His remarkable, overwhelming gift of grace to believers] is eternal life in Christ Jesus our Lord. (Romans 6:23b AMP)

Believers must be vigilant and pay attention to God. Doing this brings God's truth to us and we receive it from Him.

> So, we must listen very carefully to the truth we have heard, or we may drift away from it. For the message God delivered through angels has always stood firm, and every violation of the law and every act of disobedience was punished. So what makes us think we can escape if we ignore this great salvation that was first announced by the Lord Jesus himself and then delivered to us by those who heard him speak? And God confirmed the message by giving signs and wonders and various miracles and gifts of the Holy Spirit whenever he chose. (Hebrews 2:1-4 NLT)

Believers must keep their spiritual eyes on Him, listen to what He is saying to you, and be consistent. We are warned to listen so we don't lose interest in God and wander away into sin and unbelief. The children of Israel did not listen and ignored God. They had a relationship with God and could have entered His rest. Believers have the total forgiveness of God through Christ and the power of the Holy Spirit. In this relationship, we enter into His rest.

> And I will ask the Father, and he will give you another Advocate, He who will never leave you. He is the Holy Spirit, who leads into all truth. The world cannot receive him, because it isn't looking for him and doesn't recognize him. But you know him, because he lives with you now and later will be in you. (John 14:16-17 NLT)

How much more with the help of the Holy Spirit can we successfully serve God? *Advocate* is an older word for an attorney and is something they do – they advocate for their client. This is done through helping you through tough legal situations, complex business or personal decisions as well as many difficult things. The KJV says *Comforter* instead of *Advocate*. This word means Helper or Aid. The Holy Spirit is the *Advocate* who goes along side to help you. If God the Holy Spirit is helping you, there is no reason for fear or failure. God is on our side during challenging times and easy times, all because He loves us.

Jesus showed us that God has *greater love* for us because we are His friends.

> Greater love has no one than this: to lay down one's life for one's friends. (John 15:13 NIV)

> No one has greater love [nor stronger commitment] than to lay down his own life for his friends. (John 15:13 AMP)

This is the true, loyal love of a faithful friend who is always there for us. Jesus has a <u>greater</u> love for everyone. Because believers have entered into His love, this is our relationship with Him and our rest in Him.

When we consider Jesus, it is more than us thinking about Him. *Consider* means to observe, understand, be attentive and fix your eyes and mind upon Him. We must join together with God through our relationship. We live day-by-day, hour-by-hour with Him. He is always with us. Wherever we are, we fix our love on Him and live for Him.

> So, as the Holy Spirit says: "Today, if you hear his voice, do not harden your hearts as you did in the rebellion, during the time of testing in the wilderness, (Hebrews 3:8 NIV)

This verse says <u>do not harden your hearts</u>. This means keep your heart soft before God. Listen to Him, talk to Him and obey Him.

> See to it, brothers and sisters, that none of you has a sinful, unbelieving heart that turns away from the living God. (Hebrews 3:12 NIV)

A hard heart can occur because of an attack by the devil or the result of our rebellion towards God. Either way, we are accepting something evil that results in a bad outcome - sin. How does a believer become defeated by sin? Just stop resisting sin and we become involved. An unbelieving heart will tell us - "stop trusting God" and follow other things. In this, we ignore our relationship with God. It's as if sin will come and "knock on your door." Answering the knock on the door will let sin in. Don't do it – pay attention to God. Keep your relationship strong and active. Embrace your faith in God.

Believers have an active relationship with God. But what do we do to enter into His rest? We consider Jesus and look directly at Him using our spiritual eyes. God is a Spirit and I cannot see Him with my physical eyes, but my spiritual eyes see Him clearly. Every believer must use the spiritual "eyes of faith" from God when they pray, listen, read the Word of God and think about Him. God is greater than any difficulty we face and any temptation that comes. This is what David, Joseph and the other saints had to do though faith in God. They maintained their relationship by entering into His rest. This rest fortified them to endure the tough times they encountered.

We leave our old dead life when we enter into His relationship. New life is what we receive from God.

The old life is gone and the new life has come. Thank God.

As we enter into His rest, we experience all of His fullness and His presence. We consider Jesus, knowing that He cares for us.

Let us enter His rest through our relationship with God.

Chapter Questions

1. Hebrews 12:1 talks about a "great cloud of witnesses." How is a believer encouraged by these people of God?

2. How does "keeping our eyes on Jesus" (Hebrews 12:2) help the believer to trust God?

3. How does a believer live for God with purpose? (see page 7)

4. Why is the story of the man with many possessions (in Matthew 19:16-22) important for the believer to understand?

5. Joseph and Mary rested in God. Identify one way that they entered God's rest.

6. Martin Luther (page 9) learned that the just shall live by faith. How do you live by faith?

7. David was pursued by King Saul who wanted to capture him. Why did God call David a man after His own heart?

8. Write one scripture that showed David's character and his trust in God.

9. Write a brief answer. What is the "rest of God?"

Chapter 5

Those Who Entered God's Rest

Those who enter into God's rest seek a relationship with God and they seek to enter His rest.

> So God's rest is there for people to enter, but those who first heard this good news failed to enter because they disobeyed God. So God set another time for entering his rest, and that time is today. (Hebrews 4:6-7a NLT)

> So let us do our best to enter that rest. But if we disobey God, as the people of Israel did, we will fall. (Hebrews 4:11 NLT)

Entering His rest relies upon the believer's obedience to God. Obeying God does not earn His rest, but demonstrates faith in the relationship with God. The righteous rest in God because they trust Him. They enter into His rest because they know they will have His presence and His protection – God will always overcome.

> What then shall we say to these things? If God *is* for us, who *can be* against us? (Romans 8:31 NKJV)

The Amplified Bible (AMP) states "who can be [successful] against us?" It is a wonderful thing to be assured that God is always present, He always protects us and He will overcome.

Hebrews 11 talks about righteous people in the Old Testament who put their faith into action. These people took their faith and actively obeyed God. They understood that there is a key component to working with God - faith. They chose to believe in Him fully knowing that He is in control.

> It's impossible to please God apart from faith. And why? Because anyone who wants to approach God must believe both that he exists *and* that he cares enough to respond to those who seek him. (Hebrews 11:6 MSG)

When anyone comes to God, there is a simple requirement. Believe that He is alive (exists) and that He will respond to everyone who looks for (seeks) Him. Seeking someone who is invisible is a real stretch of human mental abilities and defies human logic. This is because people don't make contact with God with our senses, but rather we contact Him with faith. God exists and we seek our invisible God by faith.

> You will seek me and find me when you seek me with all of your heart. (Jeremiah 29:13 NIV)

> You, God, are my God, earnestly I seek you; I thirst for you, my whole being longs for you, in

> a dry and parched land where there is no water. (Psalm 61:3 NIV)

> Look to the Lord and his strength; seek his face always. (1 Chronicles 16:11 NIV)

> Keep on asking, and you will receive what you ask for. Keep on seeking, and you will find. Keep on knocking, and the door will be opened to you. (Matthew 7:7 NLT)

We seek God and He finds us. He speaks to us and opens the door to welcome us. We enter God's rest.

Abel is the first righteous man who entered into His rest.

> It was by faith that Abel brought a more acceptable offering to God than Cain did. Abel's offering gave evidence that he was a righteous man, and God showed his approval of his gifts. Although Abel is long dead, he still speaks to us by his example of faith. (Hebrews 11:4 NLT)

The full account of the two brothers Cain and Abel is found in Genesis 4:2b-9. They were the sons of Adam and Eve. "Abel kept flocks, and Cain worked the soil." (verse 2b NIV) God accepted the offering of Abel that he brought from his herds. The NLT says the "best portions of the firstborn lambs." Cain brought some of the crops he raised as an offering to the Lord. There is nothing in this text that indicates that God preferred one brother over another. There is also no mention that "a lamb is good" and "crops are bad."

I believe that Abel offered his gift to God with faith. "Abel's offering gave evidence that he was a righteous man," (NLT) The NKJV states that God testified that "through [his sacrifice] he obtained witness that he was righteous." It is necessary to believe that God exists and that He blesses people who seek Him. Abel offered his gift in faith and the sacrifice pleased God. Cain brought his offering to God in a way that did not please God. Cain might have been casual when he should have worshipped God with awe and wonder. Maybe Cain gave his offering with a sense of obligation or duty. Whatever the reason, God approved Abel's sacrifice because it was better than Cain's sacrifice.

Adam and Eve would have taught them to bring offerings to God, but Cain and Abel both approached God in a different way. Abel went to God with faith seeking to please God and Cain went to God in unbelief. Cain became extremely angry that his offering was not accepted and went on to kill Abel. Even today, the blood of Abel cries from the ground. This is the first murder in the Bible. The devil deceived their parents and now Cain was deceived into taking his anger and disappointment one giant leap further by killing his brother Abel.

I believe if Cain had gone sincerely to God in faith, God would have accepted Cain.

> "Why are you so angry?" the LORD asked Cain. "Why do you look so dejected? You will be accepted if you do what is right. But if you refuse to do what is right, then watch out! Sin is crouching at the door, eager to control you. But you must subdue it and be its master."
> (Genesis 4:6-7 NLT)

This scripture indicates that Cain did something wrong when he brought his offering, but God in His mercy wanted to make things right. This shows that Cain let his anger rule and had a hard heart to God. God spoke to Cain about his anger and doing what was right. He chose to ignore God and refused to obey. Instead of a relationship of faith and the rest of God, he decided to sin and we see the tragic outcome. Cain intentionally murdered his brother Abel.

Can a story of two brothers from many years ago be relevant to a believer today? Yes. God is eternal and timeless - faith in God gives life to anyone who reaches out to God through Jesus Christ. Believers have a relationship with God because of faith in Christ. Abel knew God and rested in Him as he humbly brought his offering. As believers approach our holy God in faith and humility, God is pleased. We no longer need to bring sacrifice a hoping to receive God's favor. Jesus brought His blood sacrifice for each of us – once and for all. In His sacrifice, we are made holy.

> For God's will was for us to be made holy by the sacrifice of the body of Jesus Christ, once for all time. (Hebrews 10:10 NLT)
>
> And in accordance with this will [of God] we [who believe in the message of salvation] have been sanctified [that is, set apart as holy for God and His purposes] through the offering of the body of Jesus Christ (the Messiah, the Anointed) once for all. (Hebrews 10:10 AMP)

Enoch was an Old Testament saint that pleased God because of his faith.

> It was by faith that Enoch was taken up to heaven without dying - "he disappeared, because God took him." For before he was taken up, he was known as a person who pleased God. And it is impossible to please God without faith. Anyone who wants to come to him must believe that God exists and that he rewards those who sincerely seek him. (Hebrews 11:5-6 NLT)

The account of Enoch's life is found in Genesis.

> Enoch lived sixty-five years, and begot Methuselah. After he begot Methuselah, Enoch walked with God three hundred years, and had sons and daughters. So all the days of Enoch were three hundred and sixty-five years. And Enoch walked with God; and

he *was* not, for God took him. (Genesis 5:21-24 NKJV)

Enoch *walked* with God for three hundred years. This means that they would walk, talk and spend time together. Enoch lived a righteous life of unbroken fellowship with God. He lived 300 years of sweet fellowship with God. Enoch followed God and dedicated his life to having and living an active relationship with Him. This brought God's blessings because Enoch sought God diligently as someone longs after a person who they desire to be with, the one they love. God came and took His friend Enoch from the earth. In this we learn that a strong close relationship with God should be the goal of every believer.

He came and took Enoch because God was pleased with Enoch. Our perfect God does perfect things.

> As for God, his way is perfect: The LORD's word is flawless; he shields all who take refuge in him. (Psalm 18:30 NIV)

Noah is best known for building the ark of God. Most everyone knows the story about Noah's Ark in Genesis 6-9.

The scriptures tell us that

> Noah was a just man, perfect in his generations. Noah walked with God. (Genesis 6:9b NKJV)

Noah was just – he was righteous and his justification came from God. People knew that there was something different about Noah. People knew that God was with him. God vindicated Noah when the flood came on the earth in judgement.

Noah was "perfect in his generations." Noah lived this as an example to his family and society. Do you mean that Noah never sinned? No, he had a relationship with God and was righteous. *Perfect* means that he had integrity, lived a life of truth as a way of life. His life was without blemish. We know that Jesus was the only sinless person, but it could be said that Noah did not live a life of casual or intentional sin. If and when he sinned, he went to God and asked forgiveness and probably offered a sacrifice to God.

Noah was a man who walked with God. This is like what was said about Enoch. This tells us of a relationship of talking and listening – they had a friendship. Friends talk about things they have in common and friends share their feelings and opinions and they laugh together. God and Noah had a living relationship.

The book of Hebrews tells us more about Noah. We learn that Noah acted in faith and that he obeyed God.

> It was by faith that Noah built a large boat to save his family from the flood. He obeyed God, who warned him about things that had never happened before. By his faith Noah

> condemned the rest of the world, and he received the righteousness that comes by faith. (Hebrews 11:7 NLT)
>
> By faith, Noah built a ship in the middle of dry land. He was warned about something he couldn't see, and acted on what he was told. The result? His family was saved. His act of faith drew a sharp line between the evil of the unbelieving world and the rightness of the believing world. As a result, Noah became intimate with God. (Hebrews 11:7 MSG)

Noah did something the world would call "crazy." Noah built a super HUGE boat. He wasn't crazy, He obeyed God. It was large. Many say about 450 to 500 feet long. That's about 1½ American football fields long. The scriptures do not tell us if the ark was by a river, if Noah was a skilled shipbuilder of if he even had the skills of a carpenter. All we know was that he walked with God and was righteous. His relationship with God turned Noah into an ark-builder. This is what he did – one of God's people was building a HUGE boat.

I realized that Noah had to invest his time and a lot of money into constructing the ark. Did he have a regular job? Did he also have to farm and tend crops? Whatever the case, Noah was devoted to living a life of service to God.

How long did the construction of the ark take? The Bible never really tells us.

Noah had to negotiate to obtain the trees that would have to be cut into boards and beams using hand tools. Pegs would have to be cut and scaffolds built. God specified it be built with "gopherwood" and covered with pitch inside and out. Pitch is a lot like asphalt and can be found in the ground or taken from heating and distilling wood. Noah's source of pitch is not mentioned in the scriptures, but it amazes me to wonder how many gallons of pitch did Noah have to obtain? This HUGE ark would have taken hundreds of board feet of gopherwood and an awful lot of pitch to coat the inside and the outside of the boat.

Due to the size and hand-built construction techniques, it would have been a monumental, time-consuming task. The completion of the ark was amazing – it took hard work and a lot of perseverance. Regardless of the challenges, Noah followed God and built the ark.

After the ark was completed, it came time for the flood to cover the face of the earth - judgement by God. God told Noah and his family to go into the boat. No one else was righteous and they would be judged by God. The wickedness of man brought God's judgement. It could be said they earned God's judgement because of their wickedness. God's judgement was their just reward. Their end was tragic but it was deserved.

> When everything was ready, the LORD said to Noah, "Go into the boat with all your family, for among all the people of the earth, I can see

> that you alone are righteous. (Genesis 7:1 NLT)

Noah had gathered all of the animals and enough food for man and beast. People tell the story of Noah and the Ark and emphasize the animals and the ark. This reduces it down to a cute children's tale. However, the Bible is different. It emphasizes three things about Noah - God's righteousness in Noah's life, Noah's walking with God and Noah's obedience to God. God had a relationship of trust with Noah and he trusted God. Noah said "YES!" to God when He told Noah to build the Ark. Noah's relationship, faith and obedience are the true emphasis of the story of Noah's life. God gave His friend Noah the plan, the reason for the boat and Noah obeyed. "Well, it looks like I am going to build a HUGE boat for God – let's get started!"

> Then the LORD closed the door behind them. (Genesis 7:16b NLT)

The flood came and covered the earth. God judged the people of the earth but Noah, his family and the animals were spared. After the flood, God brought the ark to rest on the dry ground and they all departed the ark.

> Then Noah built an altar to the LORD, and there he sacrificed as burnt offerings the animals and birds that had been approved for that purpose. And the LORD was pleased with the aroma of the sacrifice and said to himself, "I

> will never again curse the ground because of the human race, even though everything they think or imagine is bent toward evil from childhood. I will never again destroy all living things. (Genesis 8:21-22 NLT)

The Lord was happy with Noah's sacrifice – "pleased with the aroma of the sacrifice" that came from the offering. Our holy God "smelled a sweet savor" (KJV) in His nostrils from a sacrifice brought to God by a righteous man with whom He walked.

Believers can learn from Noah that God's righteousness brings a relationship with Him. This righteousness can only be received through the salvation that comes from Jesus Christ. Believers have a relationship that must be cultivated. Believers spend time with God, talk to God and listen to God because we are friends. Jesus calls us His friends. Good friends are people who love their friends.

Noah took his close relationship with God and entered into His rest. God's relationship and rest kept him during the building of the ark. I am sure that Noah was <u>the</u> controversy of the village. I am sure he took a lot of ridicule and people treated him badly. At the very least, they misunderstood Noah. All of this happened because he believed and trusted God and obeyed Him with his life.

God wants believers to learn about Noah and the importance of faith and obedience. God took his relationship with Noah in an unseen direction where no one had gone before – he followed God and built a HUGE boat! He followed through with all of the details. He gathered wood and pitch and then got to work. He gathered all of the animals, collected food and supplies and went inside the ark. Noah did all of this because the God who he believed in told him to do it. The next time that God asks you to do something that is a challenge, seems outrageous or seems impossible, remember Noah. He honored his relationship with God and obeyed.

Learning about the life and faith of Abraham would take a lifetime. He is referred to as the father of all who hold and live by faith in God.

> Therefore *it is* of faith that *it might be* according to grace, so that the promise might be sure to all the seed, not only to those who are of the law, but also to those who are of the faith of Abraham, who is the father of us all (Romans 4:16 NKJV)

Abraham's relationship with God was sealed with a covenant that was made between God and him.

> "As for me, this is my covenant with you: You will be the father of many nations. No longer will you be called Abram; your name will be Abraham, for I have made you a father of many nations. (Genesis 17:4-5 NIV)

Abram means *exalted* or *high father.* This is a title of respect that was due to his age and wisdom.

Abraham means *father* or *chief of a multitude.* From this we get a *father of many nations.* How could an old man with no children be the father of many nations? It was by faith. God promised them a child and they knew that God's promise was sure.

Abraham took God's promise, obeyed it and acted upon what God said.

> It was by faith that Abraham obeyed when God called him to leave home and go to another land that God would give him as his inheritance. He went without knowing where he was going. And even when he reached the land God promised him, he lived there by faith - for he was like a foreigner, living in tents. And so did Isaac and Jacob, who inherited the same promise. Abraham was confidently looking forward to a city with eternal foundations, a city designed and built by God. (Hebrews 11:8-10 NLT)

Abraham believed <u>in</u> God and believed <u>what</u> God had told him to do. Abraham confirmed and demonstrated his faith by leaving his home. He became a wanderer with a purpose and a destination, yet he didn't actually know God's intended destination.
Additionally, he built altars to God including the altar on which to sacrifice Isaac. These altars show a man who had a genuine relationship with God. Abraham confirmed his faith by responding to God, his friend. Abraham rested by the very act of completely trusting Him.

Abraham was able to travel about obeying God because he was expecting a city with foundations, a dwelling place with permanence for his family. It would be so much more substantial than a camp composed of people living in tents. The fulfillment of this promise is seen in ancient Israel and modern-day Israel. God promised the land to the descendants of Abraham and it is a reality today. I believe that Abraham could see this afar off because of the relationship with God. He <u>knew</u> that God would provide, even though he did not have the fulfilled promise. This is faith in the God Abraham knew.

But the question is how could he be called Abraham, meaning the *father* or *chief of a multitude* and *father of many nations*? This was because God had promised a son to Sarah and Abraham and they were confident and absolutely sure that He would give them their promised child.

> It was by faith that even Sarah was able to have a child, though she was barren and was too old. She believed that God would keep his promise. And so a whole nation came from this one man who was as good as dead - a nation with so many people that, like the stars in the sky and the sand on the seashore, there is no way to count them. (Hebrews 11:11-12 NLT)

Sarah was past her child-bearing years and was therefore too old to conceive and bear a child. Abraham was also "too old" to have children. How could God promise children to a man and woman who were past their years? Is anything too hard for God? God kept His promise and Sarah conceived. We all know the result of their faith - Isaac was born.

For all of the years of expectantly waiting for the child of promise, they would have had to live in their relationship with God and live in His rest. We could compare this example of Abraham and Sarah with a modern person who believes that God exists. They have a mental image and an understanding that there is a God. But without a relationship by faith through Jesus Christ, there is no connection to God. People must be made righteous by Christ to enter this relationship. It is more than "I believe in the existence of God." Rather, it is the type of relationship we saw with Abraham, Noah and Enoch. These are examples of people who walked with God. We walk with God and when we enter a relationship with Jesus Christ.

These people all died before they received the promise of Christ of a completed relationship of salvation, a lifetime throughout eternity with God through Jesus Christ.

> All these people died still believing what God had promised them. They did not receive what was promised, but they saw it all from a distance and welcomed it. They agreed that they were foreigners and nomads here on earth. Obviously, people who say such things are looking forward to a country they can call their own. If they had longed for the country they came from, they could have gone

back. But they were looking for a better place, a heavenly homeland. That is why God is not ashamed to be called their God, for he has prepared a city for them. (Genesis 11:13-16 NLT)

People today are disappointed when they do not accomplish the goals that they have set for themselves and die without fulfilling their dreams. Some people have established a "bucket list" of things that they want to do before they "kick the bucket" - a slang term for dying. These different people mentioned in Hebrews were not disappointed because they were righteous. They were friends of God that had a relationship with God.

Some people have more goals and some people have fewer goals. But it is the goals that come from God that demand our attention. These God-given goals are the substance that keep believers active and alive in God. Because these goals come from God, they are full of God's power.

The literal homeland for every believer is heaven where God's desires and goals are always fulfilled. On this earth, believers walk by faith in God and not by what we see or experience with our senses.

> For we walk by faith, not by sight. (2 Corinthians 5:7 NKJV)

> For we live by believing and not by seeing. (2 Corinthians 5:7 NLT)

> It's what we trust in but don't yet see that
> keeps us going. (2 Corinthians 5:7 MSG)

The fulfillment of His promises will happen in God's time. We live our very life by faith in God, not by what we see.

Some of these people died before they received the promise. Some like Noah received and lived the immediate promise – Noah and the ark God told him to build. Others did not receive the promise, yet they were righteous and lived in God's rest. They could see the promise from afar – far away in time and distance. We see this in the life of Abraham and others. They looked for better things, a heavenly homeland. Their close relationship with God was the most important thing in their life.

The Hebrew midwives and the parents of Moses were a good example of trusting God. Even though Pharaoh told them to kill all of the male babies, the midwives defied his orders. (Exodus 1) Later, Moses' parents hid him. Their trust in God showed a relationship and rest in God. During the easy times and the difficult times, God will take care of you. He took care of the Hebrew midwives and babies. He took care of Moses' parents and the baby Moses. These people took a stand of faith for God and defied the wicked decree of Pharoah.

> It was by faith that Moses' parents hid him for
> three months when he was born. They saw
> that God had given them an unusual child, and

> they were not afraid to disobey the king's command. (Hebrews 11:23 NLT)

Rahab hid the spies when they were secretly spying out Jericho. (Exodus 2)

> It was by faith that Rahab the prostitute was not destroyed with the people in her city who refused to obey God. For she had given a friendly welcome to the spies. (Hebrews 11:31 NLT)

Rahab trusted the spies sent by Joshua and trusted in the will of God. His will was for the children of Israel to conquer the city of Jericho. We could say this took courage, which it did. But in a much greater way, it an unshakeable trust in God. His rest brought courage to Rahab so she could trust and keep trusting God. Fear of the local authorities could have brought her to betray the spies. Instead, she kept their secret and trusted God. This is not an easy thing; it takes faith in God and a deep sense of His love to know He will keep us. Rahab asked the spies to give her mercy and safety for her family and they did - God provided.

In addition to these people, there are more people mentioned – people who dared to trust God. People who rested in God. People who took His promises as a literal truth. People who walked by faith and not by sight. (Hebrews 11:32-35 NLT)

But others suffered to bear their decision to trust in God. Some were tortured, whipped and killed. But they refused to renounce God.

> All these people earned a good reputation because of their faith, yet none of them received all that God had promised. For God had something better in mind for us, so that they would not reach perfection without us. (Hebrews 11:39-40 NLT)

The Greek word for a *good reputation* is based in the Greek word for *martyr*. It means to affirm that one has seen or heard or experienced something, or that he knows it because it was taught by divine revelation or inspiration. These people all earned a good reputation because they experienced and received a revelation from God. They knew that God would keep them regardless of the testing they experienced. God promised and His promise is good. This is a result of a relationship of faith and trust in God.

Believers have a relationship with God through their belief in the Lordship and resurrection of Jesus Christ. This is how salvation is received. Because they have received the promise of salvation and have a relationship, believers will be reunited with the Lord when they die or the Lord returns. This is the promise that the Old Testament saints looked for. We know that Abraham received the promised child Isaac, but he also waited.

> For he was [waiting expectantly and confidently] looking forward to the city which has foundations, [an eternal, heavenly city] whose architect and builder is God. (Hebrews 11:10 AMP)

This relationship of the believer with God is founded on better promises, because of the resurrection of Jesus Christ. We are changed spiritually into a new person because we are made into His righteousness.

The Old Testament saints <u>saw</u> the promise from a distance. Believers receive the promise.

Believers receive the Holy Spirit who was first given on the day of Pentecost. The Holy Spirit settles down to remain in the believer – actually a filling with the Spirit of God.

> And I will ask the Father, and he will give you another advocate to help you and be with you forever - the Spirit of truth. The world cannot accept him, because it neither sees him nor knows him. But you know him, for he lives with you and will be in you. (John 14:16-17 NIV)

For a believer, this is our relationship with God – God the Father, God the Son and God the Holy Spirit. The New Testament saint receives the promise and is filled with the Holy Spirit. What a wonderful blessing from God.

Christians need the rest of God to be able to follow and obey God. It's the rest that allows the believer to go forward like Noah and Abraham. This will allow the believer to accomplish God's will in your life.

Chapter Questions

1. Why is it impossible to please God without faith? (Hebrews 11:6)

2. The Old Testament saints obeyed God. (Hebrews 11) How did this help them enter into God's rest?

3. In a few words, briefly explain what happened between Cain and Abel.

4. Why was Abel righteous before God? How was he different than Cain?

5. The story of Cain and Abel is relevant today. Why is this story important for all believers to know?

6. Enoch pleased God. There are several ways he pleased God. Identify at least one of these reasons.

7. Find information about Noah and write two statements about him.

8. Noah knew God and walked with God. Describe one way that Noah demonstrated his relationship of faith in God.

9. What can a believer learn from Noah?

10. Abraham was a friend of God. What can a believer learn from studying Abraham?

11. What did God promise Abraham? Write one of these promises.

Chapter 6

Jesus Taught Us To Have A Relationship With God

The Word of God leads us to one conclusion – our life is meaningless and we are doomed if we do not surrender our life to Jesus Christ and receive Him as Lord and Savior. That is a blunt statement, but it's true.

> Then Jesus said, "Come to me, all of you who are weary and carry heavy burdens, and I will give you rest. Take my yoke upon you. Let me teach you, because I am humble and gentle at heart, and you will find rest for your souls. For my yoke is easy to bear, and the burden I give you is light." (Matthew 11:28-30 NLT)

Jesus makes it clear. We will find rest for our souls. The Message states it differently, and sheds additional light on this verse.

> "Are you tired? Worn out? Burned out on religion? Come to me. Get away with me and you'll recover your life. I'll show you how to take a real rest. Walk with me and work with me—watch how I do it. Learn the unforced rhythms of grace. I won't lay anything heavy or

ill-fitting on you. Keep company with me and you'll learn to live freely and lightly." (Matthew 11:28-30 MSG)

These words from Matthew bring a solution from God for man's problem - "how do I straighten out my life?" Jesus tells us to come to Him. If we join together with Him ("take My yoke") and receive His teaching (expert advice that will help us) we will find God. He is able and willing to help us ("we will learn to live freely and lightly" and "I will give you rest"). The answer to our problems is going to Jesus.

It helps to look at different versions of the Bible when you study. Several of the online digital Bible sites have several versions that range from the traditional King James Version to The Message, a modern personal paraphrase from the original languages. Hearing the Word of God when it is stated in a variety of ways helps me learn and understand what I am reading.

These scriptures in Matthew show us the concern that Jesus has for us. He did this so that we will go beyond a limited religious experience to an eternal meaningful relationship with God. He wants us to "be real" and share a mutual love with Him, and build on an eternal relationship with God.

Joining with Him in a relationship is easy to do. A relationship with God is a beam of light into our lives. Believers are not being burdened down with more "weight" like an Olympic weight lifter working out in the gym. Jesus wants us to enter into a rich relationship with God. He wants us to know Him in the rich blessings as well as during the tough challenges. His love for us defines His desire for a relationship with us. He has a "greater love" (John 15:13 KJV) - which is the two Greek words *megas* and *agape*. It could be said that He brings a "super BIG love of God." The love of God is preeminent in the universe because no other person or source of love equals or exceeds His love.

> Greater love has no one than this: to lay down one's life for one's friends. (John 15:13 NIV)

Our relationship with God is found in a having a relationship and spending time with Him and obeying His Word.

> Joyful are those who obey his laws and search for him with all their hearts. (Psalm 119:2 NKJV)

Obedience shows that we love God. His love for us is an established fact and was sealed by His death on the cross. Our love and our obedience for Him are the hallmark of our faith – it demonstrates our commitment and loyalty to our God. Jesus asked the apostle Peter

> "When they had finished eating, Jesus said to Simon Peter, "Simon son of John, do you love me more than these?" "Yes, Lord," he said, "you know that I love you." Jesus said, "Feed my lambs." (John 21:15 NIV)

If we love Jesus, obedience will be a natural thing.

> If you [really] love Me, you will keep *and* obey My commandments. (John 14:15 AMP)

Jesus asked Peter if he truly loved Him and told Him to help the disciples of Christ grow and mature in Him. (John 21) We love Jesus and we are happy to comply with what He tells us to do.

> Be careful that you do not refuse to listen to the One who is speaking. For if the people of Israel did not escape when they refused to listen to Moses, the earthly messenger, we will certainly not escape if we reject the One who speaks to us from heaven! (Hebrews 12:25 NLT)

> Since we are receiving a Kingdom that is unshakable, let us be thankful and please God by worshiping him with holy fear and awe. (Hebrews 12:28 NLT)

It is an act of love when we obey Him. Our obedience to God is one of the ways we worship Him. It plainly tells God that we love and respect Him and that we will surely pay the cost of serving God. "Lord, I love you and will do what you ask me to do." We worship Him as we obey and serve Him. Believers must <u>say</u> what we will do and then <u>do</u> what we say. When the believer is a "say and do" person it demonstrates character and shows a person who is resolute in what they say. We know that Peter went the full round with Jesus – he obeyed Him, helped the early church to grow and become established. Tradition tells us that Peter was crucified like Jesus, only upside down. Peter was obedient to God. He showed this commitment by what he said and did. He did it with character and a love for God.

Our obedience should be performed with love and a deep-seated respect, "a holy fear and awe" of God. We could ask – "What do we owe Him?" Everything! "How much does He love us?" Totally! "How can we ever repay Him?" We can never repay Him – it's impossible! This is why we live a life of love and respect for God. It's our joy to worship Him with obedience in our lives.

We saw His *greater love* earlier in this chapter. The ultimate way He expressed this greater love is through the salvation He earned for us and freely gives to us.

> how shall we escape if we neglect so great a salvation, which at the first began to be spoken by the Lord, and was confirmed to us by those who heard *Him,* God also bearing witness both with signs and wonders, with various miracles, and gifts of the Holy Spirit, according to His own will? (Hebrews 2:3-4 NKJV)
>
> So what makes us think we can escape if we ignore this great salvation that was first announced by the Lord Jesus himself and then delivered to us by those who heard him speak? And God confirmed the message by

giving signs and wonders and various miracles and gifts of the Holy Spirit whenever he chose. (Hebrews 2:3-4 NLT)

Salvation is a free gift from God. The word *escape* refers to running away any type of disobedience to God. The context of *escape* is taking a risk of missing out on the offer of God's salvation because "transgression and disobedience [will receive] a just reward." A choice has to be made between living a life of sin or receiving life from Christ. The smart choice (and only real choice!) is to obey God and become a believer through Christ.

Not obeying God results in many things – unbelief, a hard heart, wicked behavior, etc. This clearly tells us that disobedience is a bad thing that opposes God. The apostle Paul (who was then called Saul) was disobedient when he arrested and persecuted believers because he did not know God's salvation in Christ.

> You know what I was like when I followed the Jewish religion—how I violently persecuted God's church. I did my best to destroy it. (Galatians 1:13 NLT)

Jesus got Saul's (Paul's) attention on the road to Damascus – he knocked him to the ground and spoke to him. Jesus asked "why are you persecuting Me?" Saul reached out and received salvation through Jesus. Instead of neglecting the salvation, Saul paid attention to Jesus, obeyed Him and began a lifelong relationship with God. The relationship was personal and close. The nature of the relationship is very evident in the epistle, the letters he wrote to the churches.

When people neglect His salvation, they become careless. The person really doesn't care about God. They could "care less" and have no concern for God. They live their life as if God doesn't exist or that He is unconcerned about people.

The *great salvation* (Hebrews 2:3-4) can be best described by what Jesus did in the Gospels. He rose from the dead and redeemed mankind. Jesus healed people from diseases and delivered them from demons. He raised the dead and promised eternal life to those who received Him as Lord. We see what Jesus said about His relationship with the Father. Jesus told people that with Him that all people could have a relationship with the Father.

> Jesus answered, I am the way and the truth and the life. No one comes to the Father except through me. (John 14:6 NKJV)

Jesus said that going to Him could be compared to going through a narrow gate, where the number of people is limited because the gate is small. In contrast, the way to eternal destruction is a wide highway where many people to walk at the same time. We can see this in the difference between a small path and a wide interstate highway.

> You can enter God's Kingdom only through the narrow gate. The highway to hell is broad, and its gate is wide for the many who choose that way. But the gateway to life is very narrow and the road is difficult, and only a few ever find it. (Matthew 7:13-14 NLT)

These scriptures both tell us that it is only through Jesus Christ that we can enter a relationship with God and receive eternal life. This choice must be made by everyone – eternal life with God or eternal and permanent destruction in hell. These scriptures clearly tell the importance of a relationship with God and the way to Heaven.

Believers must consider their relationship with God as an ongoing permanent connection that grows. We are called to abide in a constant love for God and people. This means we must persevere and actively work within our relationships with God and those around us. There are times that the opposition and temptation to quit becomes a real challenge. This is the time to make a decision to "keep on keeping on", dig our heels into the ground and resist the temptation to quit.

> Let us hold tightly without wavering to the hope we affirm, for God can be trusted to keep his promise. Let us think of ways to motivate one another to acts of love and good works. And let us not neglect our meeting together, as some people do, but encourage one another, especially now that the day of his return is drawing near. (Hebrews 10:23-25 NLT)

We look unto Jesus, the author and finisher of our faith (Hebrews 12:2 NKJV). The NLT tell us that "We do this by keeping our eyes on Jesus, the champion who initiates and perfects our faith." Jesus starts our faith and grows and improves our faith in God that is within us. He was tempted to quit but He persevered because He loved and obeyed God. Even today, He has a deep unquenchable love for us. We can look to Him for help and know He will help us in our time of need.

Jesus remained constant in God and resisted sin. He relied on His relationship with the Father. When He was in the Wilderness (Matthew 4:1-11 NIV), He resisted the devil with the Word of God. Jesus could have fallen to the temptation and committed sin against God. Instead, He honored the Father with obedience and rested firmly in His relationship with God.

When we become Christians, we enter a relationship with God through Jesus Christ. The Bible tells us that believers are a new creation in Christ.

> Therefore, if anyone *is* in Christ, *he is* a new creation; old things have passed away; behold, all things have become new. (2 Corinthians 5:17 NLT)

Our new life *in Christ* means that we are also in the Father. Because of Jesus we are united with the Father.

> My Father, who has given them [disciples, believers] to Me, is greater than all; and no one is able to snatch them out of My Father's hand. I and My Father are one. (John 10:30 NKJV)

We are held tightly in the Father's hand. This is the keeping power of God. This allows for every believer to have has a relationship with God that is personal and dear. God loves us, He keeps us and we have a relationship with Him. What a wonderful and amazing thing!

The Father promised that He would send God the Holy Spirit to be with us.

> And I will ask the Father, and he will give you another Advocate, who will never leave you. He is the Holy Spirit, who leads into all truth. (John 14:16-17a NLT)

> I am going to send you what my Father has promised; but stay in the city [Jerusalem] until you have been clothed with power from on high. (Luke 24:49 NIV)

> When the day of Pentecost came, they were all together in one place. Suddenly a sound like the blowing of a violent wind came from heaven and filled the whole house where they were sitting. They saw what seemed to be tongues of fire that separated and came to rest on each of them. All of them were filled with the

> Holy Spirit and began to speak in other tongues as the Spirit enabled them. (Acts 2:1-4 NIV)

The Holy Spirit given to believers is the promise of the Father. The Holy Spirit lives within us and fills us to the top. He is the presence of God within every believer. We are aware of Him in our lives. We will learn to rely upon Him when He comes to abide with us. This is not a promise for the future, but is a part of our relationship with God today.

The Holy Spirit empowers us to share Jesus with people, to love people and to do the works that He did. Jesus shared the good news of the Father, inviting people to "come home because God's not mad." The Father welcomes us home when we come to Him through Jesus. God welcoming us home can be seen when the father of the prodigal welcomed his son home with rejoicing and a celebration. (Luke 15:11-32 NIV)

> For this son of mine was dead and is alive again; he was lost and is found. So they began to celebrate. (Luke 15:24 NIV)

> In the same way, there is more joy in heaven over one lost sinner who repents and returns to God than over ninety-nine others who are righteous and haven't strayed away! (Luke 15:7 NLT)

> The LORD your God is with you, the Mighty Warrior who saves. He will take great delight in you; in his love he will no longer rebuke you, but will rejoice over you with singing. (Zephaniah 3:17 NIV)

> In the same way, I tell you, there is joy in the presence of God's angels over one sinner who repents. (Luke 15:10 NIV)

God is so happy when a sinner repents and turns over the control of his life to God. He and the angels rejoice. I am sure there is a shout in Heaven with lots of singing. "They have come home! YAY! Praise God for His mercy!"

We are disciples and students of Jesus. We have a relationship with Him. The people in the Gospels refer to Jesus as Teacher and Master. This denotes respect to him that occurs in a teacher/pupil relationship. Believers are students of Jesus with a desire to learn everything about Him! We learn many things from our teacher including who God is, His nature and character and His great love for us.

Our relationship with our Teacher brings a desire to obey Him. We live our love for Jesus when we obey from Him and learn from Him.

> If you love me, keep my commands. (John 14:15 NIV)

> If you [really] love Me, you will keep and obey My commandments. (John 14:15 AMP)

It has always amazed me that so many people walk away from accepting Jesus and His resurrection. But I had the exact same attitude and reaction before I was saved. I remember that Jesus was calling me to receive Him and I said "no" or "not right now" more than once.

> the Spirit of truth, whom the world cannot receive, because it neither sees Him nor knows Him; but you know Him, for He dwells with you and will be in you. (John 14:17 NKJV)

> the Spirit of Truth, whom the world cannot receive [and take to its heart] because it does not see Him or know Him, but you know Him because He (the Holy Spirit) remains with you continually and will be in you. (John 14:17 AMP)

The Holy Spirit within us prompts and reminds us to follow, trust and obey God. I can often "hear" a scripture or a simple "do this" – I "hear" these promptings deep down in my spirit, not with my ears. I can sense when God is telling me to do something. I cannot explain it, but I can sense His presence. I pray that you too would hear from God. Him speaking to each of us is life changing and shows us the personal nature of our relationship with Him.

Jesus talks about His love for the Father.

> But that the world may know that I love the Father, and as the Father gave Me

> commandment, so I do. Arise, let us go from here. (John 14:31 NKJV)

The love that the Father and Jesus have for each other cannot be explained because it goes above and beyond any love that we know. We could say His love "is off the charts." God's love is the greatest love that ever has or ever will exist. The Father loved us when we were unrighteousness when we were not able or allowed to legally approach God. Jesus Christ loved us so much that He was tortured and died personally for each of us. He endured this suffering and knows each of us by name because of His great love for us.

> Greater love has no one than this: to lay down one's life for one's friends. (John 15:13 NIV)

The Father gave up His Son to be made sin and was then sacrificed Him for each of us. Jesus suffered a horrible death to purchase our redemption. The is love that is cannot be measured in human terms. Jesus showed us the greatest love of all times.

Several scriptures from Isaiah 53 will bring this love to light. This Old Testament prophecy shows how God sacrificed Jesus out of a deep love for us.

> Surely he took up our pain and bore our suffering, yet we considered him punished by God, stricken by him, and afflicted. But he was pierced for our transgressions, he was crushed for our iniquities; the punishment that brought us peace was on him, and by his

wounds we are healed. We all, like sheep, have gone astray, each of us has turned to our own way; and the LORD has laid on him the iniquity of us all. (Isaiah 53:4-6 NIV)

He was oppressed and afflicted, yet he did not open his mouth; he was led like a lamb to the laughter, and as a sheep before its shearers is silent, so he did not open his mouth. (Isaiah 53:7 NIV)

Yet it was the LORD's will to crush him and cause him to suffer, and though
the LORD makes his life an offering for sin, (Isaiah 53:10a NIV)

I will give him the honors of a victorious soldier, because he exposed himself to death. He was counted among the rebels. He bore the sins of many and interceded for rebels. (Isaiah 53:12 NLT)

Jesus had the punishment inflicted upon Him by God and took the harsh suffering we deserved. Think about it, He was punished, stricken and afflicted and then pierced with a spear in the side. He was silent while being beaten. He was "crushed like a grape" to make Him suffer. During His life, He went through extreme hardship to win our freedom. He was a hero and at the same time He took the hit for us. This is who we have a deep and grateful relationship of love with. Thank Jesus for what He did for us.

Man sinned against God yet Jesus willingly carried this sin to the cross so that we could be forgiven. Someone had to be sacrificed and it was only the sinless, perfect Jesus who could legally take our punishment. "He bore the sins of many and interceded for the rebels" – He "stepped into our sin" and went to the Father for us. He did all of this because He loved us and still loves us now.

Our relationship with Him is unshakeable and leads us to become closer to Him.

> Teach me to do your will, for you are my God. May your gracious Spirit lead me forward on a firm footing. (Psalm 143:10 NLT)

> I can of Myself do nothing. As I hear, I judge; and My judgment is righteous, because I do not seek My own will but the will of the Father who sent Me. (John 5:30 NKJV)

> Jesus said to them, My food is to do the will of Him who sent Me, and to finish His work. (John 4:34 NKJV)

> He went on a little farther and bowed with his face to the ground, praying, My Father! If it is possible, let this cup of suffering be taken away from me. Yet I want your will to be done, not mine. (Matthew 26:39 NLT)

Doing the will of the Father and following Him is the most important thing in a believer's life. Jesus received his life and nourishment from God. He set the example for us by demonstrating the importance of following God. This example encourages us to follow His example. The excellent free advice we receive from Jesus is this - follow God and obey Him.

Hardhearted people refuse to follow God. These are the people who actively resist Him.

> And the Father who sent me has testified about me himself. You have never heard his voice or seen him face to face, and you do not have his message in your hearts, because you do not believe me—the one he sent to you. (John 5:37-38 NLT)

This type of refusal is common in our society. Today, many people seek a multitude of different pleasures instead of seeking and knowing God. They're too busy, too concerned with their money or possessions, they elevate another god above the true God and some just plain do not believe that God exists, many because they cannot see Him with their physical eyes.

> Only fools say in their hearts, "There is no God." They are corrupt, and their actions are evil; not one of them does good! (Psalm 14:1 NLT)

> The [spiritually ignorant] fool has said in his heart, "There is no God." They are corrupt, they have committed

> repulsive *and* unspeakable deeds; There is no one who does good. (Psalm 14:1 AMP)
>
> For the message of the cross is foolishness to those who are perishing, but to us who are being saved it is the power of God. For it is written: "I will destroy the wisdom of the wise; the intelligence of the intelligent I will frustrate." (1 Corinthians 1:18-19 NIV – scripture portion quoted from Isaiah 29)
>
> Since God in his wisdom saw to it that the world would never know him through human wisdom, he has used our foolish preaching to save those who believe. (1Corinthians 1:21 NLT)

In contrast, people who are wise and have a relationship with God live a rich life of thankfulness to God. The believer says with a thankful heart, "I know and worship the living God. I am thankful for Jesus and that I have a relationship with God!" This clearly shows wisdom in a person who appreciates their relationship with God. What a great difference between the foolish person who denies God and the wise person who embraces God!

In the same way that God-deniers rebel against God, Israel constantly tested God through their rebelliousness. Right after they left slavery and bondage in Egypt, they started to complain about the food God provided. They had been freed from Egyptian slavery and yet complained about what they were eating.

One of their problems was that the years of bondage in Egypt reprogrammed their thinking. They were changed from the children of Israel to common slaves who only understood servitude to a cruel Egyptian master. They were freed from slavery and were restored to their God-ordained position of life with God. Christians are often locked into a mentality of servitude to the world and the devil. The Word of God tells us what to do after we enter a relationship with God.

> throw off your old sinful nature and your former way of life, which is corrupted by lust and deception. Instead, let the Spirit renew your thoughts and attitudes. Put on your new nature, created to be like God—truly righteous and holy. (Ephesians 4:22-24 NLT)

Through this renewal, believers enter a personal relationship between God and us. Part of this relationship is reading, studying and thinking about God and His Word. Believers live in a community of faith through attending and becoming involved in a local church. It is through these internal and external things that we love, praise and work together with God.

Believers work together with God and they are changed into the likeness of God by the Holy Spirit. We all look different, but we have the same Holy Spirt inside of us and we all have a personal relationship with the same God.

> And we all, with unveiled face, *continually* seeing as in a mirror the glory of the Lord, are *progressively* being transformed into His image from [one degree of] glory to [even more] glory, which comes from the Lord, [who is] the Spirit. (2 Corinthians 3:18 AMP)

The Word of God transforms us as we read and learn it. We grow in God as we absorb it and as we grow, we are changed into a new and different person. It's more than attending a class or taking an online course, it involves each believer receiving and developing a relationship with Him. God reveals His truth and the meaning of knowing Him. As the believer surrenders to the Lord and grows in Him, the relationship grows stronger and deepens.

I surrendered my life to the Lord and received Him as Savior while reading a Billy Graham book. My relationship grew as I prayed, read the Word of God and attended church. God became real to me and He changed me into His image. It has taken time, but it's well worth it. Everyone has the opportunity to develop a relationship with Him as you seek and find Him and yield yourself to Him. Believers can grow up as they follow and obey the Lord.

> So let us stop going over the basic teachings about Christ again and again. Let us go on instead and become mature in our understanding. Surely, we don't need to start again with the fundamental importance of

> repenting from evil deeds and placing our faith in God. (Hebrews 6:1 NLT)

> Rather, you must grow in the grace and knowledge of our Lord and Savior Jesus Christ. All glory to him, both now and forever! Amen. (2 Peter 3:18 NLT)

Every believer has a relationship with God and grows into His strength.

> But those who wait on the LORD Shall renew *their* strength; They shall mount up with wings like eagles, They shall run and not be weary, They shall walk and not faint. (Isaiah 40:31 NKJV)

When God renews our strength, it becomes apparent in our lives in a variety of ways. The believer can develop a new understanding of the Word of God that allows you to worship God and share Christ in a greater way. This renewed strength can take the form of a physical healing. A believer can receive moral strength to withstand criticism, hatred or temptation. The renewal of this strength comes from *waiting* on the Lord. *Wait* means looking for God's, keeping your hope in God and expecting Him to help you. Hope is an expecting confidence in God, which says "I know that God will bless and help me."

We orient our lives to be on God's time. God is never late, but He always arrives on time. God is love and an all-powerful God, not a tardy God who doesn't care. He knows what He is doing which means that believers trust Him with an unshakeable confidence. This trust is "faith in action" in the life of the believer.

This results in the believer loving God and having a desire for His presence in their lives.

> As the deer pants for streams of water, so my soul pants for you, my God. My soul thirsts for God, for the living God. When can I go and meet with God? Why, my soul, are you downcast? Why so disturbed within me? Put your hope in God, for I will yet praise him, my Savior and my God. (Psalm 42:1-2, 5 NLT)

> Love the LORD, all you godly ones! For the LORD protects those who are loyal to him, but he harshly punishes the arrogant. So be strong and courageous, all you who put your hope in the LORD! (Psalm 31:24-25 NLT)

> We love Him because He first loved us. (1 John 4:19 NKJV)

This love for God motivates us grow and increase our relationship with Him. His love is constant. It is a natural thing to want to love people like our spouse, our children, our families and friends. However, it is a challenge to love the unlovable. People are unpredictable and can disappoint us, but God does not change – He is love and will always be love. When our "soul thirsts for God" we can know that our desire and love are well aimed and we are safe in our relationship with Him. Rightfully we put our hope in Him. The believer who trusts in God will never be disappointed.

We cherish our relationship with God as a precious possession. We stay loyal to Him in our relationship – not to earn His love but to thank Him for His love to each of us. Being loyal involves us actively living faithful to God which we learn in our relationship with Him. Jesus was always loyal and faithful to God in spite of the temptation to quit. In spite of this opposition and daily abuse, He triumphed and knew God was with Him.

> Don't be afraid, for I am with you. Don't be discouraged, for I am your God. I will strengthen you and help you. I will hold you up with my victorious right hand. (Psalm 41:10 NLT)

> Don't panic. I'm with you. There's no need to fear for I'm your God. I'll give you strength. I'll help you. I'll hold you steady, keep a firm grip on you. (Psalm 41:10 MSG)

There are times that I allow myself to become fearful. I know better than to do this, but I become overwhelmed in spite of what I know is written in God's Word. We saw "Don't panic. I'm with you." Believers that are overwhelmed need to come to their spiritual senses and decide to trust God. This is why our relationship with God and other believers is so important – we can turn to God and His Body (the

Church). The Church is made up of believers that provide support, help and prayer when we receive opposition, are sick and face challenging problems.

In spite of what happens in the life of a believer, God never tosses us aside or refuses to help us. He will never leave or forsake us.

> Be strong and courageous. Do not be afraid or terrified because of them, for the LORD your God goes with you; he will never leave you nor forsake you. (Deuteronomy 31:6 NIV)

> Be strong. Take courage. Don't be intimidated. Don't give them a second thought because GOD, your God, is striding ahead of you. He's right there with you. He won't let you down; he won't leave you. (Deuteronomy 31:6 MSG)

Confidence in God comes when we become aware of the scriptures that tell us that God is there for us – personally and individually. This is His love demonstrated lavishly to us. His everlasting presence in our lives changes us and helps us grow in Him. Believers walk confidently in His love when we know Him in a close relationship.

We have a living relationship with Him. He changes us when we bring ourselves to Him offering ourselves in worship.

> Therefore, I urge you, brothers and sisters, in view of God's mercy, to offer your bodies as a

> living sacrifice, holy and pleasing to God—this is your true and proper worship. Do not conform to the pattern of this world, but be transformed by the renewing of your mind. Then you will be able to test and approve what God's will is—his good, pleasing and perfect will. (Romans 12:1-2 NIV)

When we bring ourselves to Him, we approach Him in a worshipful and respectful manner. As always, we know who God is and we know our position – we are in Christ. All that we are and all that we hope to ever be is because of Him. In light of these facts and our position in Christ, it is a normal thing that <u>we</u> bring ourselves to God as a living sacrifice just as Jesus brought Himself to God to suffer and die upon the cross. Should believers also bring ourselves to God as a sacrifice? A wholehearted YES!

We do not adapt ourselves to be like the world. We choose a different way, a different course of action. We choose "the Way" Jesus Christ.

When we enter a relationship with God, the first thing that a new believer notices is how different things are. Old things have died and gone away and everything has become new – the old is gone and the new has come. (2 Corinthians 5:17b paraphrase) I can clearly remember the day I was saved – I am sure that the day looked normal, but somehow it seemed brighter. My car wouldn't start – no big deal. I went to see the local "Jesus people" and found out I was born again. This was something new to me. I began my lifelong journey of a relationship with God. Anyone who chooses to be in Christ is a brand new creation made by God (2 Corinthians 5:17a paraphrase). I was raised in church, but being born again and the newness I could feel was a real surprise. I was actually in a relationship with God Almighty! It was very different because God didn't seem far away; I knew He was now my friend.

This new relationship brought the transforming power of the Word of God and made my mind new. Old thinking was gone. The new "God thinking" was here. My life was being changed one new Bible-based thought at a time. I knew my old life had been lived in opposition to God. This was clear. But now I could see the Truth of Jesus Christ as I followed His new Way and lived a new Life in Him.

> Jesus answered, "I am the way and the truth and the life. No one comes to the Father except through me. If you had really known me, you would know who my Father is. From now on, you do know him and have seen him!" (John 14:6-7 NIV)

> Jesus said, "I am the Road, also the Truth, also the Life. No one gets to the Father apart from me. If you really knew me, you would know my Father as well. From now on, you do know him. You've even seen him!" (John 14:6-7 MSG)

Our wonderful Savior, Jesus Christ gave all believers a relationship with a loving Father. Jesus lived it, taught it and gave it to each of us personally.

> God saved you by his grace when you believed. And you can't take credit for this; it is a gift from God. (Ephesians 2:8 NLT)

Thank God for His wonderful gift. He gave us His Son, our Lord and Savior Jesus Christ.

Chapter Questions

1. Jesus told us that He will give us rest. Read Matthew 11:28-30 and write one or more ways that people receive rest from Him.

2. What are one or more things that people must do to receive His rest?

3. In Psalm 119:2, believers are told to obey and seek God. Briefly describe how <u>you</u> obey and seek Him.

4. Love and obedience to God is a form of worship. What things do you do to love and obey God?

5. Briefly describe your salvation experience when you received Jesus as Lord and Savior and began an eternal relationship with Him.

6. Jesus is the only way to get to God for salvation. Why is the narrow gate in Matthew 7:13-14 a good analogy for people receiving Christ?

7. What did Jesus do to resist the temptation of the devil in the Wilderness? (Matthew 4:1-11)

8. Following Jesus and the will of the Father is the most important thing in anyone's life. How does a believer do this?

9. How do rebelliousness and denying God contribute to someone refusing a relationship with God?

10. How do following and obeying God contribute to a great relationship with God?

11. Why is it important to be involved in a local church?

12. Briefly describe how the Word of God changes the believer.

13. Isaiah 40:31 talks about renewing our strength. What happens in the life of a believer when they *wait* upon the Lord?

14. When you became a believer, what was one of the "new" things you noticed after your conversion? (2 Corinthians 5:17)

Chapter 7

God's Covenant With Man

The covenant between God and the believer is an eternal relationship that Jesus earned by means of His personal sacrifice on the cross of Calvary. He ministers to His people through this covenant.

> But now Jesus, our High Priest, has been given a ministry that is far superior to the old priesthood, for he is the one who mediates for us a far better covenant with God, based on better promises. (Hebrews 8:6 NLT)

> But as it is, Christ has acquired a [priestly] ministry which is more excellent [than the old Levitical priestly ministry], for He is the Mediator (Arbiter) of a better covenant [uniting God and man], which has been enacted *and* rests on better promises. (Hebrews 8:6 AMP)

> But Jesus' priestly work far surpasses what these other priests do, since he's working from a far better plan. If the first plan—the old covenant—had worked out, a second wouldn't have been needed. (Hebrews 8:6 MSG)

Jesus earning our redemption reminds a believer that it is useless for people to struggle and work hard to get to God.

Similar to the concept of "hard work gets us to God," the concept of "my good deeds must outweigh my bad deeds" is not accurate because it is not found in the Bible. It is only Jesus' redemption on Calvary that buys our freedom from sin and our wonderful relationship with God. We receive eternal life because of Jesus, not because of doing more good things than bad things.

Hebrews clearly states that the New Covenant that Jesus brought from God is of a greater or more excellent quality than the Old Covenant that God gave to Israel. This is the Law that the Levitical priesthood administered. The covenant of Jesus was a more excellent covenant because it was based on better promises.

Today, a covenant usually refers to property restrictions. In the Bible, a covenant is an agreement made between two parties. This covenant agreement is different – it comes with promises. In the case of the book of Hebrews, *covenant* refers to the two agreements that were made between God and man. The first covenant mentioned was made between God and the children of Israel at Mt. Sinai. The second covenant was made with Jesus. Believers are made a part of the new, second covenant. This is because at the new birth the person becomes a believer and every believer has all that is in Christ.

There are two very different covenants. The Old Covenant is based on the Law that God gave to Moses when the children of Israel were in the

Wilderness. God delivered them from bondage in Egypt and brought them into the Wilderness to establish a relationship with them. This relationship was made between God and the entire nation of Israel - with each individual citizen of Israel.

The New Covenant is based the death and resurrection of Jesus Christ. His sacrifice bought all people freedom from the bondage to sin. They were released from eternal death and brought into eternal life.

The Old Covenant was based on obedience to the Law.

> Now therefore, if you will indeed obey My voice and keep My covenant, then you shall be a special treasure to Me above all people; for all the earth *is* Mine. (Exodus 19:5 NKJV)

This covenant between God and Israel brought blessings for obedience to the Law or curses for disobedience. In some cases, sin was committed by an individual and they were punished.

The basis of the covenant was obeying God through completely following all of the Law. The Law could never be successfully followed by someone because God was dealing with imperfect human beings who were born in sin – they could not obey because they had a sin nature. Sin is the normal way of life for people.

God saw the pitiful condition of man because there was no way that they could be forgiven of sin. They could never totally obey God's Law and earn their forgiveness. All of the sacrifices there were made in the Temple could never pay the penalty of sin. Instead, the sacrifices reminded the people of their sinfulness and their need for a solution from God.

> But instead, those sacrifices actually reminded them of their sins year after year. For it is not possible for the blood of bulls and goats to take away sins. (Hebrews 10:3-4 NLT)

Israel was God's "special treasure" who dearly needed relief and release from sin. God did a new thing – He sent His Son Jesus Christ to earth to save mankind. This is the New Covenant of Jesus Christ.

> "The days are coming," declares the LORD, "when I will make a new covenant with the people of Israel and with the people of Judah. It will not be like the covenant I made with their ancestors when I took them by the hand to lead them out of Egypt, because they broke my covenant, though I was a husband to them," declares the LORD. "This is the covenant I will make with the people of Israel after that time," declares the LORD. "I will put my law in their minds and write it on their hearts. I will be their God and they will be my people. No longer will they teach their neighbor, or say to one another, 'Know the LORD,' because they will all know me, from the least of them to the

> greatest," declares the LORD. "For I will forgive their wickedness and will remember their sins no more." (Jeremiah 31:31-34 NIV)

This same scripture is repeated by the writer of Hebrews.

> And they will not need to teach their neighbors, nor will they need to teach their relatives, saying, 'You should know the LORD.' For everyone, from the least to the greatest, will know me already. (Hebrews 8:11 NLT)

> When God speaks of a "new" covenant, it means he has made the first one obsolete. It is now out of date and will soon disappear. (Hebrews 8:13 NLT)

The Old Covenant was a burdensome and impossible covenant for man to keep, so God made it obsolete. He made a New Covenant with man. It was no longer an external set of rules and regulations because it would now be put in the minds of the people and "written" upon their hearts. God would now make His high standards an internal truth within His people.

The holy Law of God is now resident inside of us. We know it and it's a part of us. Since people now have a relationship with God and know His Law, they want to follow and obey God. His Law tells us do not murder, do not steal, etc. My heart and life have been changed and the new desire is to follow God.

No longer would obedience to the Law be the exclusive way to have a relationship of righteousness with God. Instead, people could now be fully justified and have a relationship with God because of the sacrifice of Jesus Christ.

> For God so loved the world that he gave his one and only Son, that whoever believes in him shall not perish but have eternal life. For God did not send his Son into the world to condemn the world, but to save the world through him. (John 3:16-17 NIV)

> This is how much God loved the world: He gave his Son, his one and only Son. And this is why: so that no one need be destroyed; by believing in him, anyone can have a whole and lasting life. God didn't go to all the trouble of sending his Son merely to point an accusing finger, telling the world how bad it was. He came to help, to put the world right again. (John 3:16-17 MSG)

The scripture teaches us that God loved all of the people of the world with a passionate, unfailing love. He sent Jesus on a mission – to seek and save the lost. In this, He provided a means to save the people of the world. This is still true today; He still loves with this same love. Man can receive this eternal life and be one with God forever. This is our covenant relationship with God – a close relationship that is eternal. We are in Christ and one with God forever.

What a great and wonderful thing that God initiated and did for us!

How do we know this is true? It lies in the fact that God took an oath and it is impossible for Him to lie.

> People swear by someone greater than themselves, and the oath confirms what is said and puts an end to all argument. Because God wanted to make the unchanging nature of his purpose very clear to the heirs of what was promised, he confirmed it with an oath. God did this so that, by two unchangeable things in which it is impossible for God to lie, we who have fled to take hold of the hope set before us may be greatly encouraged. (Hebrews 6:16-18 NIV)

This is an important scripture because it demonstrates that God always tells the truth. He is telling us the importance of always speaking truth. This tells us that God tells the truth so we tell the truth."

People take an oath when they testify in court. A solemn promise is made that we will give the complete truth in our testimony. The oath-taker places their hand on the Bible to affirm their oath with the words, "so help me God." This sets a serious tone for the oath and reminds the person to tell the truth during their testimony.

God took an oath that He would bless Abraham and make him a great nation. This is true because God Almighty took an oath. We know it is true because He does not and cannot lie. His Word is His bond, the guarantee of the promise of His truth.

This is our God, the God that we trust and live for. This is the God that we put our hope in. Plainly stated, you can trust God.

Our trust of salvation and a relationship with God is not dependent upon our obedience to the Law. People cannot completely keep the Law. This means that the Law is ineffectual – it just does not work when people become a part of the equation. God's Law is holy and perfect. People are not. To fix man's problem, God sent Jesus to rescue us - He "straightened us out." He set our feet on a sure path so we could now follow Him with an established heart.

> The former regulation [the Law] is set aside because it was weak and useless (for the law made nothing perfect), and a better hope is introduced, by which we draw near to God. And it was not without an oath! Others became priests without any oath, but he became a priest with an oath when God said to him: "The Lord has sworn and will not change his mind: 'You are a priest forever.'" Because of this oath, Jesus has become the guarantor of a better covenant. (Hebrews 7:18-22 NIV)

> a former commandment is cancelled because of its weakness and uselessness [because of its inability to justify the sinner before God] (for the Law never made anything perfect); while on the other hand a better hope is introduced through which we now *continually* draw near to God. And indeed it was not without the taking of an oath [that Christ was made priest] (for those *Levites* who formerly became priests [received their office] without [its being confirmed by the taking of] an oath, but this One [was designated] with an oath through the One who said to Him, "THE LORD HAS SWORN AND WILL NOT CHANGE HIS MIND *or* REGRET IT, 'YOU [Christ] ARE A PRIEST FOREVER'"). And so [because of the oath's greater strength and force] Jesus has become the certain guarantee of a better covenant [a more excellent and more advantageous agreement; one that will never be replaced or annulled]. (Hebrews 7:18-22 AMP)

The Word of God tells us that the Law had weaknesses because it could not save people. People who tried to keep the Law still had distance between them and God because of sin.

Jesus provided a better hope, as well as a new and better way to trust God. Man could now receive salvation and a relationship with God. His oath and His truthfulness guaranteed it – He made salvation and a relationship a sure thing and a "done deal!" His

157

resurrection and His blood secured our salvation. God made us righteous through our Savior Jesus Christ.

> He made Christ who knew no sin to [judicially] be sin on our behalf, so that in Him we would become the righteousness of God [that is, we would be made acceptable to Him and placed in a right relationship with Him by His gracious lovingkindness]. (2 Corinthians 5:21 AMP)

> For God made Christ, who never sinned, to be the offering for our sin, so that we could be made right with God through Christ. (2 Corinthians 5:21 NLT)

He became sin by taking our sin upon Himself. Jesus was the only righteous and sinless person who could die and offer His blood to totally wash the human race clean from sin. This is a demonstration of the pure love that God has for every person. God is perfect and His love is perfect. He clearly shows His love through the sacrifice of Jesus for everyone everywhere.

Under the Law, people could not be saved and washed from their sin. Total forgiveness was not possible. But because of Christ, we are completely forgiven and freed from sin.

> so also Christ was offered once for all time as a sacrifice to take away the sins of many people. (Hebrews 9:28a NLT)

This is the New Covenant that Christ brought to us. We receive a new life purchased for us by God through the sacrifice of Jesus Christ.

Because of the New Covenant, we are now close to God. Jesus calls us His friends. (John 15:15 NIV) We are now His companions. This statement about our friendship with God comes while Jesus is sharing in John 15 about the relationship between the vine and a branch.

We all know that a branch can only live and produce fruit while it is connected to the vine. Cut off the branch from the vine and it will have BIG problems! The cut-off vine demonstrates that the believer cannot live our lives and produce fruit for God unless we have a relationship with Jesus. The more we trust God and rely upon Him, the more we will be satisfied and the more we will produce fruit. Our fruit is our sharing the Kingdom of God with people as a result of the Holy Spirit working in our lives. We now produce "the fruit of the Spirit [which] is love, joy, peace, forbearance, kindness, goodness, faithfulness, gentleness and self-control." (Galatians 5:22-23 NIV) This fruit is a result of our relationship with God. The fruit that we produce is brought by the Holy Spirit in our lives. We work together with Christ and the Holy Spirit helps us to produce fruit. It's all in our relationship with God just like the branch and the vine – Jesus the True Vine. (John 15)

Paul asked the Galatian church "how they could be satisfied by starting a relationship with God and then try to live the relationship through following the Law?"

> I ask you again, does God give you the Holy Spirit and work miracles among you because you obey the law? Of course not! It is because you believe the message you heard about Christ. (Galatians 3:5 NLT)

The believers in the Galatian church began their Christian life normally - following Christ and the New Covenant. They then decided that they wanted to change and follow God through life under the Old Covenant. They started a relationship with God and He showed them grace and mercy. Somewhere they changed to a "works" relationship where every person had to earn God's favor through performance. Which covenant do you want – receive His favor or earn His favor? And don't forget, earning God's favor is impossible.

> The old system under the law of Moses was only a shadow, a dim preview of the good things to come, not the good things themselves. (Hebrews 10:1a NLT)

The priests in the Old Testament offered sacrifices under the Law. These sacrifices showed obedience and submission to God as well as a relationship of total and reliance upon God. Sacrifices honored God as <u>their</u> God and were done to obey the Law. But the sacrifices did not erase sin. The Galatian church wanted to return to the Law and follow it, thinking that following the Law would earn the blessings and favor of God.

God ended the first covenant and yet the Galatians wanted to go backwards and live under the Old Covenant. Jesus came to do what God wanted – He obeyed God because of His relationship with the Father. Jesus fulfilled the Old Covenant and brought the New Covenant so we could follow God.

> Then he said, "Look, I [Christ] have come to do your will." He cancels the first covenant in order to put the second into effect. For God's will was for us to be made holy by the sacrifice of the body of Jesus Christ, once for all time. (Hebrews 10:9-10 NLT)

Jesus brought the New Covenant to the world. He came to do God's will and tell the people that there was now a way to be forgiven from sin and have a relationship with God. In the four Gospels, the Jewish religious leaders argued with Jesus in the same way that the people had argued with Moses. In spite of their covenant with God, they refused the good news that Jesus brought from God.

> You study the Scriptures diligently because you think that in them you have eternal life. These are the very Scriptures that testify about me, yet you refuse to come to me to have life. (John 5:39-40 NIV)

The Jews had a covenant with God and they should have been the ones who listened to God. But their hearts were hard – they believed their own manmade religious opinions instead of believing what God was trying to tell them. When God sent prophets to bring messages of correction and encouragement, they killed them. When God sent Jesus, the hard-hearted religious leaders ignored Him, arrested Him and turned Him over to the Romans for crucifixion. Their actions were the result of having a hard heart – a heart that resists and refuses God. A heart that says "NO!" to a relationship with God.

> If only you would listen to his voice today! The LORD says, "Don't harden your hearts as Israel did at Meribah, as they did at Massah in the wilderness. For there your ancestors tested and tried my patience, even though they saw everything I did. (Psalm 95:7b-9 NLT)

The Lord tells us to <u>not</u> harden our hearts like Israel did. Rather, we should be diligent and on guard to be sure that we are trusting God. We must keep our hearts tender to His correction and encouragement. Believers are people that have a relationship with God. Having a relationship means that we warmly welcome our friend and do things that build our relationship. A soft heart welcomes God and nurtures a relationship with Him.

In the same way that Israel <u>could not enter</u> the Promised Land because of rebellion and unbelief, we <u>can enter</u> into His promises for us through obedience and belief in Jesus Christ. When we cooperate and work together with God on His timetable, we enter His promises for us. This is our relationship with God. He leads and we follow.

The choice in this chapter comes down to which of the covenants will you choose? Will you choose the Old Covenant and following the Law or the New Covenant and following Jesus Christ? The Law has already been given to the world. If we do not choose Jesus and the New Covenant, this "non-choice" brings you the Law and it becomes your choice by default.

The other choice of covenants is the New Covenant and Jesus Christ. In mentioning this, I am giving you the good news – Jesus Christ is the only true answer for each and every person in the world.

You either totally obey His Law or you give yourself completely to Christ. These are the two covenants and your choice is demanded. Making no choice brings the default - death. The choice of Jesus Christ brings eternal life through the New Covenant. Choose Jesus.

> "I am the way and the truth and the life. No one comes to the Father except through me. If you really know me, you will know my Father as well. From now on, you do know him and have seen him." (John 14:6-7 NIV)

Choose Jesus. Choose His New Covenant. Choose Life.

Chapter Questions

1. Jesus earned man's redemption. Why is it useless for people to work hard so they can try to get to God?

2. What is a covenant? Why is a covenant important?

3. Briefly describe the Old Covenant.

4. Briefly describe the New Covenant.

5. Why is the New Covenant a <u>better</u> covenant?

6. The holy Law of God is now resident inside of us. (Hebrews 8:11) Briefly explain the changes that occur with the believer.

7. God swore an oath. What is an oath and why is this important?

8. Without Jesus, man could now receive salvation and a relationship with God. How did Jesus secure our salvation and a relationship with God? Why is His redemptive work absolutely necessary?

9. In John 15, our relationship with God is compared to a vine and a branch. Why is this a good comparison? How does it show our absolute dependence upon God?

10. When a believer decides to try to live under the Old and New Covenant together, it does not work. Why?

11. Why does a hard heart make it difficult for a person to love, obey and serve God?

12. Briefly describe one new thing you learned in this chapter.

Chapter 8

A Relationship With Moses and Christ

A *spoiler alert* is needed when you are about reveal a football score or a movie ending to someone who does not know the results. We really shouldn't tell someone the outcome because it *spoils* the anticipation of knowing how something finishes.

Here's a *spoiler alert* for this chapter – a relationship with Christ is better than one with Moses. This spoiler alert is really a simple but important idea to consider.

Let's look at Moses first. Exodus 33 describes the personal relationship that God had with Moses.

> And so the LORD used to speak to Moses face to face, just as a man speaks to his friend. (Exodus 33:11a AMP)

To say that the relationship with Jesus is *better* does not mean that one relationship is good and one is bad. *Better* means *more excellent*. Both relationships are good and both relationships are of God. But what we see here is that the relationship with Jesus is of a greater value and a greater magnitude than a relationship with Moses. Both are good but one is better. Clearly, the relationship with Jesus is greater than a relationship with anyone else. We can live in a relationship that is described as the "greater love" Jesus has for us.

We know that Christ had a close relationship with the Father. They were so close that they were one – "I and my Father are one." (John 10:30 NIV) Jesus was one with the Father in all things. They were one in their dedication to the mission of saving all people and one in making people righteous so they could be one with God in Christ. The sacrifice of Jesus would change everything that ever was and that would ever be. Man could now have a close, personal and eternal relationship with God. Christ was one with God and because of Jesus, man could now enter that relationship and be one with God.

Moses and Christ had a relationship with God. Their lives motivate us to enter a relationship with God and know Him.

Both Moses and Jesus understood that God was on their side – He would protect and keep them regardless of what happened. Whether it was something regular or something BIG, God would always be there.

> But I trust in your unfailing love; my heart rejoices in your salvation. I will sing the LORD's praise, for he has been good to me. (Psalm 13:5-6 NIV)

We know that both of them went through some really tough situations – Moses and the children of Israel were backed up against the Red Sea with Pharaoh chasing them co he could recapture them. Instead of being paralyzed by fear, Moses trusted God. Jesus spent His entire ministry opposed by the religious leaders who despised Him. They were working hard to discredit and eliminate Him. Jesus had to constantly resist the evil opposition. In this, He knew that God was on His side – God was "for Him."

> So, what do you think? With God on our side like this, how can we lose? (Romans 8:31 MSG)

This is what Moses and Jesus understood clearly. They could both take stock and live their lives based on the support of God. If God said it, they could both trust Him and act with confidence.

Moses and Christ triumphed because they had a relationship with God. This is how they withstood the seemingly impossible trials they experienced in life and still stayed connected to God.

> O LORD, oppose those who oppose me. Fight those who fight against me. Then I will rejoice in the LORD. I will be glad because he rescues me... [and I] will thank you in front of the great assembly. I will praise you before all the people ...proclaim your justice, and... praise you all day long. (Psalm 35:1, 9, 18, 28 NLT)

Both Moses and Jesus brought the people to God. Moses brought people to God through the Law that God gave to Israel. He introduced them to God and led them through the desert. Neither Moses nor the first generation of Israel entered the Promised Land because of their rebellion and disobedience. Jesus Christ brought us to God through the good news of the Gospel and His Word given to each of us. We received eternal salvation through believing and accepting His resurrection from the dead. Because of Jesus, we enter the believer's "Promised Land" of an eternal relationship with God.

The relationship Moses had with God came because he was one of the children of Israel, a descendant of Abraham. The relationship of God and Moses changed and intensified when God confronted Moses in the desert at the burning bush. God called Moses to serve Him and do things that would be impossible except for God's presence and intervention.

> There the angel of the LORD appeared to him in flames of fire from within a bush. Moses saw that though the bush was on fire it did not burn up. (Exodus 3:2 NIV)

> When the LORD saw Moses coming to take a closer look, God called to him from the middle of the bush, "Moses! Moses!" "Here I am!" Moses replied. "Do not come any closer," the LORD warned. "Take off your sandals, for you are standing on holy ground. I am the God of your father - the God of Abraham, the God of

Isaac, and the God of Jacob." When Moses heard this, he covered his face because he was afraid to look at God. (Exodus 3:4-6 NLT)

Our holy, loving God called Moses and told him that He would deliver His people from the harsh and cruel slavery of Egypt. God used Moses to bring about His plan to free His people. Moses would be sent as God's ambassador to Pharoah to proclaim their freedom. God would strike Pharaoh extremely hard and perform wondrous miracles through Moses to bring them freedom. They would be freed from Egypt by God to live with and worship God in the wilderness. God would accomplish all of this using His friend Moses.

Jesus Christ the Word of God had a relationship with God that always existed.

> In the beginning was the Word, and the Word was with God, and the Word was God. (John 1:1 NKJV)

> In the beginning [before all time] was the Word (Christ), and the Word was with God, and the Word was God Himself. (John 1:1 AMP)

From these examples about Moses and Christ, believers can clearly understand the absolute necessity of a relationship with God. Moses could only go to Pharoah in Egypt with the divine presence of God leading and keeping him. In this it was clear that God definitely kept Moses. Earlier Moses had tried to help the people of Israel by killing a cruel Egyptian slave driver. This serious crime caused him to have to flee Egypt as a murderer and a fugitive from Egyptian law.

The authority and miracles that came in Egypt were a result of the power and presence of God with Moses. God and Moses went together to Pharoah because they had a relationship.

> But Moses said to God, "Who am I that I should go to Pharaoh and bring the Israelites out of Egypt?" (Exodus 3:11 NIV)

> But Moses protested to God, "Who am I to appear before Pharaoh? Who am I to lead the people of Israel out of Egypt?" (Exodus 3:11 NLT)

The gravity of the situation of returning to Egypt was clear to Moses. Without God, he was just another common criminal in Egypt. In Egypt he was unable to approach Pharaoh. With God, Moses was an ambassador sent by God.

God came to Egypt to work miracles and bring freedom to His people through Moses. He knew that it was God alone who gave Him the authority and power to confront and triumph over Pharoah. With God alone, he could lead the people out of Egypt. God told Moses that the sign or proof of God sending him would be the entire nation worshipping at the mountain of God. God did what He said He would do.

When we read this, we see the reality and truth of a relationship with God.

Jesus lived fully within His relationship with God His Father. It is an insufficient statement to say that a relationship with God is important. A relationship with Jesus so much more than important because this is the only Way to get to God. Access to the Father only comes through Jesus Christ. (John 14:6) Jesus came to help us receive eternal life, not to condemn us to a life of eternity in hell. (John 3:16-17) Believers will receive a personal and permanent relationship with God through trusting Christ. The relationship is promised to all, but it is only received from God by faith.

Moses was a prophet sent by God to Pharaoh and Israel. Moses brought the message that God wanted them to hear and did the works that He wanted them to see. The role of Moses as a prophet for God was similar to what we later saw in the prophets Elijah and Elisha.

God sent His son Jesus to speak the words that God wanted spoken and do the works He wanted done. He came on a mission from God that was completely successful.

> I will raise up for them a prophet like you from among their fellow Israelites, and I will put my words in his mouth. He will tell them everything I command him. (Deuteronomy 18:18 NIV)

> Then he said to the disciples, "Anyone who accepts your message is also accepting me. And anyone who rejects you is rejecting me. And anyone who rejects me is rejecting God, who sent me." (Luke 10:16 NLT)

> When God raised up his servant, he sent him first to you to bless you by turning each of you from your wicked ways. (Acts 3:26 NIV)

Jesus was the Son of God and was sent as a prophet from God to bring the message of God. The dictionary states that a *prophet* is someone who is an inspired teacher and tells the will of God. The *prophet* is inspired by the Spirit of God to bring the message to the people. Using this definition, Jesus was a prophet sent by God, but He was so much more than a prophet. He was the Messiah of God sent by God to save His people from their sins.

> She will give birth to a Son, and you shall name Him Jesus (The LORD is salvation), for He will save His people from their sins. (Matthew 1:21 AMP)

His mission was expanded and fulfilled beyond that of an Old Testament prophet. Jesus was the Messiah and Son of God who was the sinless and perfect sacrifice of God. He came in a human body and was 100% human and 100% God. (John 1:1, Colossians 2:9)

Moses was born an Israelite but was raised in the house of Pharaoh. This made him a prince in the royal family. Jesus Christ is the Son of God and came to earth as a baby born to Mary in Bethlehem.

We read this about Moses.

> And the child grew, and she brought him to Pharaoh's daughter, and he became her son. So she called his name Moses, saying, "Because I drew him out of the water." (Exodus 2:10 NKJV)

And about Christ, we read this.

> He will be great, and will be called the Son of the Highest; and the Lord God will give Him the throne of His father David. And He will reign over the house of Jacob forever, and of His kingdom there will be no end." (Luke 1:31-32 NKJV)

Jesus will return to earth as the "King of all kings and Lord of all lords." (Revelation 19:16 NLT) Jesus is God and therefore vastly superior to all of the princes and prophets that ever existed. Jesus is all-powerful and earthly kings have no authority unless it comes from God. The rulers might think they are "high and mighty" in this world, but they are brought low in submission before God.

When both Moses and Jesus were babies, they were almost killed by the government officials and soldiers. This evil was inspired by the devil and carried out to eliminate God's chosen servants. They tried to stop the promise of God to the people of the earth.

> Then Pharaoh gave this order to all his people: "Every Hebrew boy that is born you must throw into the Nile, but let every girl live." (Exodus 1:22 NIV)

> After the wise men were gone, an angel of the Lord appeared to Joseph in a dream. "Get up! Flee to Egypt with the child and his mother," the angel said. "Stay there until I tell you to return, because Herod is going to search for the child to kill him." Herod was furious when he realized that the wise men had outwitted him. He sent soldiers to kill all the boys in and around Bethlehem who were two years old and under, based on the wise men's report of the star's first appearance. Herod's brutal action fulfilled what God had spoken through the prophet Jeremiah:

>> "A cry was heard in Ramah - weeping and great mourning. Rachel weeps for her children, refusing to be comforted, for they are dead." (Matthew 1:13, 16-18 NLT)

This threat of murder of Moses and Jesus was made by two kings who were motivated and used by the devil. God protected both of these babies so they could fulfill their destiny from God. "No Moses" means no deliverance from the bondage of Egypt for Israel.

"No Jesus" means no sacrifice to bring God's gift of salvation for the entire human race. But our mighty God would not be stopped by two evil kings who rebelled against God. Again, and always – GOD WINS!

> O LORD, oppose those who oppose me. Fight those who fight against me. Then I will rejoice in the LORD. I will be glad because he rescues me... [and] will thank you in front of the great assembly. I will praise you before all the people ...proclaim your justice, and... praise you all day long. (Psalm 35:1, 9, 18, 28 NLT)

Today, believers must take these examples of the power of God to preserve and keep Moses and Jesus as something that is a "now" thing. History is true, but "now" is a part of our lives today. God will keep His people and bring about His will regardless of the challenge at hand. These examples of Moses and Jesus directly apply to the people of God today. God will always keep you and never leave or forsake you! Our holy God does not quit and He always triumphs! We give praise to our God for His love, His mercy and His keeping!

It is easy to sit and read these historical examples that we see in our Bible. Reading is good, but we must actively believe and live what we read about God. Believers must mix the scriptures with faith (Hebrews 4:2 NKJV) to be able to gain and live in the promises of God. Our life with God is more than our knowledge about God, it is a living and personal relationship with Him. During our reading, believers must pay particularly close attention to Jesus. He is the starter and completer of our faith. He is seated at the right hand of God and goes to God for each of us.

> Therefore, holy brothers and sisters, who share in the heavenly calling, fix your thoughts on Jesus, whom we acknowledge as our apostle and high priest. He was faithful to the one who appointed him, just as Moses was faithful in all God's house. Jesus has been found worthy of greater honor than Moses, just as the builder of a house has greater honor than the house itself. For every house is built by someone, but God is the builder of everything. "Moses was faithful as a servant in all God's house," bearing witness to what would be spoken by God in the future. But Christ is faithful as the Son over God's house. And we are his house, if indeed we hold firmly to our confidence and the hope in which we glory. (Hebrews 3:1-6 NIV)

The scriptures give us these examples of Moses and Jesus so we can actively follow them. Believers must focus on Jesus Christ, the Son of God. We are told to pay close attention and think about Him.

The KJV tells us to *consider* Jesus. This means more than having an occasional thought that He lived many years ago in the Middle East, or that He was an important historical religious figure. *Considering* Him means that we fully observe Him in our thoughts and our beliefs. We see Him in our mind's eye, our conscious thoughts as we "see" Him. As I write this, I cannot see Jesus with my physical eyes. But I can behold Him with my heart and in my mind and discover more about Him as I learn and spend time in His presence. I can truly know Him on a personal level – a one-on-one relationship. He becomes first in my priorities. He is "now" in my life, not some distant fleeting thought. *Considering* Him means we cherish and value His person, His desires for us and know Him in His suffering and resurrection.

It is easy to see the faithfulness of Moses to God and Israel. He felt the suffering of his "real family" the Israelites as they suffered and toiled in Egypt as slaves. Moses was faithful to God when he returned to Egypt to confront Pharaoh as God's representative. Moses spoke, God acted and God delivered. He delivered His beloved children out of bondage and to a relationship with Him. God called, rescued and prepared His people. Believers can receive this deliverance and relationship in Jesus Christ.

Jesus Christ was faithful to God and has a greater honor than Moses. His honor is greater because He is God and created all things as we read in John 1. In the same way as the house builder is greater and outshines the house that is built, Jesus outshines the many sincere faithful servants of God. We read about the servant's lives and can see God's presence and intervention. We can look down through the ages and see these people faithfully serving God. Jesus came to do God's will and in all of His doing, He suffered and bought redemption and righteousness that is available to all people everywhere.

Christ is the faithful Son over God's house. We become His house when we go to God with confidence and hope through faith in Jesus Christ. God lives in us and is a permanent resident who will never leave us. We can sing, "everyday with Jesus is sweeter than the day before" and know it as our way of life in Him. My life is now great and grows even better each day. I am in Christ and He is in me. His blessings are a free gift of God!

Moses suffered for God as he served Him. He knew it was a better choice to follow God than to live a luxurious but empty life without God. Moses had a choice – he could ignore or acknowledge God. Moses chose God.

> He thought it was better to suffer for the sake of Christ than to own the treasures of Egypt, for he was looking ahead to his great reward. It was by faith that Moses left the land of Egypt, not fearing the king's anger. He kept right on going because he kept his eyes on the one who is invisible. (Hebrews 11:26-27 NLT)

> He considered the reproach of the Christ [that is, the rebuke he would suffer for his faithful obedience to God] to be greater wealth than all the treasures of Egypt; for he looked ahead to the reward [promised by God]. By faith he left

> Egypt, being unafraid of the wrath of the king; for he endured [steadfastly], as seeing Him who is unseen. (Hebrews 11:26-27 AMP)

Moses acknowledged God and accepted the personal cost that he would pay for following God in his life. He knew he was a rich man because of the presence of God and the relationship that he had with God. When God got ahold of Moses, he was a criminal living in the middle of nowhere in the desert as a shepherd. His life was changed from that of a shepherd to that of the deliverer of God's people. With God, all things are possible.

> Jesus looked hard at them and said, "No chance at all if you think you can pull it off yourself. Every chance in the world if you trust God to do it." (Matthew 19:26 MSG)

The suffering of Christ was infinitely greater than the suffering that Moses endured. There is really no comparison between the suffering of Moses and Jesus. However, we thank and praise God that they both followed and obeyed God. The suffering, death and resurrection of Jesus Christ bought and brought our justification, our healing and made us righteous in Christ before God. This wonderful work was done by Christ. You and I had nothing to do with this but to accept it. Again, we see that man received this free gift from God. Not *earned* it, but received it.

> who Himself bore our sins in His own body on the tree, that we, having died to sins, might live

> for righteousness—by whose stripes you were healed. (1 Peter 2:24 NKJV)

Believers are faced with the choice of a relationship with Moses and the Old Covenant of the Law or we can choose a relationship of faith in God with Jesus Christ and life in the New Covenant.

When these choices are presented, it is critical that we make the right choice – we choose God's New Covenant through Jesus Christ. It is only through Christ that we can approach God, that we can have a close relationship with God and that we can receive eternal life. The choice is clear – it's choose God or choose nothing.

The world and the devil offer the empty choices in the "choose nothing" option. "Empty" means that there is no substance contained in it. Choosing the empty choice is like an invisible air sandwich – there is nothing there to eat for lunch! Every time we do the math, we see that nothing plus nothing equals nothing. Choose Christ – choosing Him brings a life of substance from God.

> This day I call the heavens and the earth as witnesses against you that I have set before you life and death, blessings and curses. Now choose life, so that you and your children may live and that you may love the LORD your God, listen to his voice, and hold fast to him. For the LORD is your life, and he will give you many years in the land he swore to give to your

fathers, Abraham, Isaac and Jacob.
(Deuteronomy 30:19-20 NIV)

The spoiler alert we mentioned earlier is a very real thing. But it involves more than a football game or a new movie. It involves our own personal lives and asks "where will we spend eternity?" Moses told Israel when they were faced with the big choices of life to choose God.

God chose us and sent His Son Jesus for us. We can live eternally with God starting today *if* we receive Him as our Lord and Savior. The choice is very clear – "choose life so that you your children may live." In making this choice, we became a believer in Christ and begin a rich life of loving God. We obey Him and cherish Him because we are now one with Him.

Today is the day of choices. Choose Jesus.

Chapter Questions

1. Briefly describe one thing about God's relationship with Moses.

2. Why is a relationship with Jesus better than a relationship with Moses?

3. We know that Jesus had a close relationship with His Father. Describe at least one aspect of this relationship. If possible, quote a scripture to support your answer.

4. What is your motivation for growing and developing your relationship with God?

5. How could Moses go to Pharoah and demand the release of Israel from the bondage of slavery?

6. What is a *prophet*? How was Moses a prophet? How was Jesus a prophet?

7. Why should believers consider and concentrate on Jesus (Hebrews 3:1)?

8. In what ways were the sufferings of Jesus greater than the sufferings of Moses?

9. How does a believer *consider* Jesus? (Hebrews 3:1-6)

10. Moses and Jesus were threatened with death as a baby. Why did the authorities try to kill them?

11. Both Jesus and Moses were faithful to God. Briefly describe how they were faithful.

12. Moses chose to obey God rather than to live a life of luxury in Egypt. Why was Moses' decision the *better* choice?

13. Why were the sufferings of Jesus more significant than Moses' sufferings?

Chapter 9

A Relationship With The Body of Christ

The Body of Christ is exactly that – the earthly body of the resurrected Jesus Christ who is now seated in heaven. The Body is made up of the members of the Church, those righteous men and women who have received Jesus Christ as their Lord and Savior.

> But our bodies have many parts, and God has put each part just where he wants it. How strange a body would be if it had only one part! Yes, there are many parts, but only one body. (1 Corinthians 12:18-20 NLT)

> All of you together are Christ's body, and each of you is a part of it. (1 Corinthians 12:27 NLT)

Becoming a member of the Body of Christ is not the same thing as joining a church – applying for membership and then start attending. Those who are members of the Body of Christ are justified and enter His Body through faith in the risen Christ. This justification is received by faith from Christ.

> For in it the righteousness of God is revealed from faith to faith; as it is written, "The just shall live by faith." (Romans 1:17 NKJV)

> This Good News tells us how God makes us right in his sight. This is accomplished from start to finish by faith. As the Scriptures say, "It is through faith that a righteous person has life." (Romans 1:17 NLT)

The righteous become part of the Body of Christ by faith – just or righteous people live by their faith in God. They become alive for eternity when they join the Body because they receive new life. All of this is done through faith in God.

Jesus constantly demonstrated His faith and reliance upon the Father in the Gospels. His close relationship with God was a sure thing that He demonstrated time after time.

> I and the Father are one. (John 10:30 NIV)

> For in Christ lives all the fullness of God in a human body. (Colossians 2:9 NLT)

These scriptures clearly show us that Jesus was one with God. This is true in the fact that He is God, but also true in the fact that He demonstrated to us that He lived in a close relationship with God. Believers can learn this truth from Jesus – stay close to God.

> In that day you will know that I am in my Father, and you in me, and I in you. (John 14:20 ESV)

We are in Christ; we are part of His Body and we are one with God. We do not deserve this wonderful relationship within ourselves. It is all because of Christ and His resurrection.

Because we are members of the Body of Christ, we are members of His Church. The Church goes beyond all denominational groups, beyond the written history of the church and beyond the lives of individual people. The Church is eternal and directly connected with God.

As members of the Body of Christ, we function in service to Christ while new are here on earth. We are here as the spiritual Body doing God's business – seeking and saving the lost.

> Keep on loving each other as brothers and sisters. Don't forget to show hospitality to strangers, for some who have done this have entertained angels without realizing it! Remember those in prison, as if you were there yourself. Remember also those being mistreated, as if you felt their pain in your own bodies. (Hebrews 13:1-3 NLT)

This text clearly shows us our responsibility as members of His Church. We are in God's family, our Father in heaven and all of His children. Some of the family are in heaven and some on earth. (Hebrews 12:1a) Family members cheer each other on with encouragement, love each other and help each other. We remember those in prison with prayers and practical ministry. People who are mistreated are some of those in need – the homeless, single-parent families and the abused. Regardless of their circumstances we need to be aware of them and "feel their pain" when <u>we</u> act to help them.

This is what a church should be doing – we love God and we love people. We have faith and works that go together with our belief in God. These are all things that He does for the people on earth in cooperation with His Body. This is the Gospel of Jesus Christ in action.

We are the family of God. These family relationships are found with believers that are within the Church – the worldwide church, the local church and the church within our own flesh and blood families. The Church that makes up His Body are those blood-washed saints that Jesus died for and rose from the dead to redeem. This is what it means to be a *Christian.* Church membership has value, but a believer is one who believes and accepts Jesus Christ as Lord and Savior. A believer is literally "born again" into the Family of God.

> "I will live in them and walk among them. I will be their God, and they will be my people. Therefore, come out from among unbelievers, and separate yourselves from them, says the LORD. Don't touch their filthy things, and I will welcome you. And I will be your Father, and you will be my sons and daughters, says the LORD Almighty." (2 Corinthians 6:16b-18 NLT)

People are not born-again Christians just because they are born and raised in a Christian family or they grow up in church. Receiving Jesus is a separate decision made by each person when they are old enough to understand their need for God, mature enough to comprehend accepting Christ. Jesus clearly told us that a person <u>must</u> be born again. "Very truly I tell you, no one can see the kingdom of God unless they are born again." (John 3:3 NIV) *Must* means "you gotta do it!"

The responsibility of the believer is to grow in God and know God through Jesus Christ. To do this, every believer needs to become a part of a local congregation of the Body of Christ. Within this local family, believers grow in God and learn about Him. Our relationship with God is also with His Body. Believers are born into His family by faith.

God tells believers to not remain angry at people. Instead, love your neighbor – people inside and outside of the Church. (Leviticus 19:18) Believers are known by their love – their desire and ability to be kind to others even when it is not easy or convenient. Jesus said that our love for other people sets us apart as His followers. (John 13:35) A church is a place of refuge where God's love reigns. This love goes out into the community and the world as believers carry Christ to everyone.

> A new command I give you: Love one another. As I have loved you, so you must love one another. (John 13:34 NIV)

> Love must be sincere. Hate what is evil; cling to what is good. Be devoted to one another in love. Honor one another above yourselves. (Romans 12:9-10 NIV)
>
> Greater love has no one than this: to lay down one's life for one's friends. (John 15:13 NIV)

The love of God is what makes His Church different. God's love is not the passive love we see in some poetry. God's love is active. The ultimate act of love was God sending Jesus to His death and sacrifice Him to pay for the sins of mankind. Because of this sacrifice, all people can come to God and be one with Him. This is why Jesus told His disciples to go everywhere and preach the good news to everyone. God continually reaches out to all people by His Holy Spirit and His love brings people to Christ.

A family shows love for each other within the relationship. Family love and loyalty even occurs where there are problems and challenges within imperfect families. God desires and actively seeks relationships with broken, imperfect people who are in desperate need of God's love in their lives.

When faced with God's love, someone might would ask, "Do you mean me?" Jesus always answers "Yes!" He demonstrated His "greater love" by the cruel death He suffered for every person. His death and resurrection were an act of His personal love for each person that has continued down through the ages to the people who are alive today.

Believers need each other. Likeminded people in politics and philosophy seek each other out to accomplish mutual goals. The Body of Jesus Christ cooperates to move forward together and bring the message of God to all – He loves us! In this, we are bringing the will of God. Believers are not an organization or a movement, but rather the blood-washed Church of Jesus Christ.

The Church transcends man-made groups who share purpose because we are born again. We are actually transferred from spiritual death of our old man to spiritual rebirth of our new man. We are totally new people in Christ – all of the old is gone and is replaced by a completely new "us." (2 Corinthians 5:17 paraphrase) This is the good news of Christ that we bring to a desperate world that is separated from God. It is a lost and dying world in need of new life.

Believers are blended into local congregations and fellowships and are joined and supported by the Holy Spirit.

> So now you Gentiles are no longer strangers and foreigners. You are citizens along with all of God's holy people. You are members of God's family. Together, we are his house, built on the foundation of the apostles and the prophets. And the cornerstone is Christ Jesus himself. We are carefully joined together in him, becoming a holy temple for the Lord. Through him you Gentiles are also being

> made part of this dwelling where God lives by his Spirit. (Ephesians 2:19-22 NLT)

Churches bring the saints together for meaningful worship of the risen Lord, teach the saints the Word of God and bring the saints together to interact and work together as a family. Churches are so much more than a religious social club. Churches are the spiritually alive family of their Father fitted together into <u>the</u> Body of Christ.

> And let us consider one another in order to stir up love and good works, not forsaking the assembling of ourselves together, as *is* the manner of some, but exhorting *one another,* and so much the more as you see the Day approaching. (Hebrews 10:24-25 NKJV)

> Let's see how inventive we can be in encouraging love and helping out, not avoiding worshiping together as some do but spurring each other on, especially as we see the big Day approaching. (Hebrews 10:24-25 MSG)

The role and function of the local church is set by God for us to live our lives in Christ. Believers are the Body of Christ.

> For as the body is one and has many members, but all the members of that one body, being many, are one body, so also *is* Christ. (1 Corinthians 12:12 NKJV)

The human body is composed of many individual and unique parts. This means that everyone is different. Believers are also all different, but together we become one because we belong to God.

Believers are called to work together because we are one in Christ. Common purpose is seen in our love for God and our love for people. This is true in our individual lives as believers and moreso in our mutual love that occurs inside the church and outside the church.

> Let all *that* you *do* be done with love. (1 Corinthians 16:14 NKJV)

The life of the believer is in Christ. Together, our Christian family carries and lives the good news of Christ. Our support for each other grows when we work together to weather and triumph in adversity. We lean on each other and we support each other.

The Salvation Army is based on the support that Christ brings to the Church as we live for and serve Christ together. In the 1800's, William Booth worked the streets of London to bring lost souls to Christ, with over 1,000 volunteer workers and evangelists. They ministered to the down and out – "thieves, prostitutes, gamblers, and drunkards were among their first converts to Christianity. And soon, those converts were also preaching and singing in the streets as living testimonies to the power of God." These radical converts supported each other as the military supports each other – they were an army for the Lord.

(The Salvation Army – salvationarmyusa.org) Believers today still bring a radical message of Christ rescuing people from death and bring them to Christ to receive new life.

It is the power of the risen Christ that binds believers together. We are one in Christ in unity and purpose. When the Church works together in Christ, we become people who "turn the world upside down." (Acts 17:6 NKJV) Believers who cooperate and follow the Scriptures offer the world a message of faith, salvation and unity. Believers have a genuine relationship with the Lord.

> Behold, how good and how pleasant *it is* for brethren to dwell together in unity! *It is* like the precious oil upon the head, running down on the beard, the beard of Aaron, running down on the edge of his garments. *It is* like the dew of Hermon, descending upon the mountains of Zion; for there the LORD commanded the blessing - life forevermore. (Psalm 133 NKJV)

New converts need support, regardless if the support comes from a church or a Christian ministry. As parents nurture and raise their babies into childhood and beyond, the church is charged with this task to help all believers to grow in Christ.

> Fathers, do not provoke your children to anger by the way you treat them. Rather, bring them

> up with the discipline and instruction that
> comes from the Lord. (Ephesians 6:4 NLT)

It is ridiculous to think of a baby changing their own diaper and preparing their own bottle before they struggle to climb into their crib to sleep. A baby won't yell across the house, "Don't worry about me Mom – I'm doing just fine." Instead, we hear a cry in the middle of the night from our babies that is a cry for help – feed me, change me, hold me. But how can the Church expect the young converts to raise themselves? The Church is responsible help the young Christian "with the discipline and instruction" of being a believer as they grow and increase in their understanding of the Word of God.

A strong local body of Christians experience peace within themselves. This peace that comes from Christ is what we offer to the lost. Jesus Christ personally living within each us gives us peace that allows us to live a victorious, "go forward" life in Christ.

> Peace I leave with you; my peace I give you. I do not give to you as the world gives. Do not let your hearts be troubled and do not be afraid. (John 14:27 NIV)

Jesus gives His people perfect unending peace. His peace is "now" - it's for today. His peace lasts for eternity. The believer's soul is at peace because of their relationship with Christ and with His body. We do not have to live in fear because God is for us. Jesus gave us His peace and therefore believers are safe, content and satisfied with their new life in Christ. We are new creations! What more could anyone ask or desire?

Believers are known as people who love God and show love to people. Christians can show love because they have a relationship with God through Christ.

> My command is this: Love each other as I have loved you. (John 15:12 NIV)

Jesus demonstrated God's love for us in many different ways. Friendliness, kindness, compassion for the down and out and for the sick, etc. But Jesus gave more, He came to earth to offer Himself. He was innocent and sinless – the perfect and only acceptable sacrifice for <u>our</u> sin. He forgave us, He delivered us, He protected and He brought healing to the sick. This was true on the day He died and was resurrected and it is true today. By His stripes we were healed. (1 Peter 2:24 KJV) People were cured, healed, made whole and delivered to God by salvation. This still applies today.

> walk in the way of love, just as Christ loved us and gave himself up for us as a fragrant offering and sacrifice to God. (Ephesians 5:2 NIV)

Live a life filled with love, following the example of Christ. He loved us and offered himself as a

> sacrifice for us, a pleasing aroma to God.
> (Ephesians 5:2 NLT)

People talk about the importance of young people having a good role-model to follow. Jesus was the perfect role model for all people to follow, but He was more than a role-model. He was a perfect and sinless human as well as the divine Son of God. We can look to Him as a *perfect* (not just *good*) example for our lives and we can allow the risen Christ to live and act through us. We love and worship God and we love and help people. He commanded that we do this. Regardless of someone's faults and imperfections, we love them. In the church, we love people and work together with them. I love God and therefore I love people. This implements the truth that God is love.

Love is work and is definitely a sacrifice. In the same way that there is a personal cost to serve God, there is a personal cost to love some people. Face it, some people are basically tough to love – it is a sacrifice to love them. Jesus chose to love us. He came to earth and died knowing that we were unlovable people in severe need. He knew that unsaved people are unrighteousness and cannot approach and get to God without Christ. Still, He came to earth to love us and He still loves us today. God is love.

> So let's not get tired of doing what is good. At just the right time we will reap a harvest of blessing if we don't give up. Therefore, whenever we have the opportunity, we should

> do good to everyone—especially to those in the family of faith. (Galatians 6:9-10 NLT)
>
> So let's not allow ourselves to get fatigued doing good. At the right time we will harvest a good crop if we don't give up, or quit. Right now, therefore, every time we get the chance, let us work for the benefit of all, starting with the people closest to us in the community of faith. (Galatians 6:9-10 MSG)

Love is the rule for all believers. It starts at home within our family and those close to you. Paul told us in Galatians that we should particularly love those in our church family. Love will help believers to move beyond simple problems like the color of carpet in the church building. Love will help believers to confront big problems that divide families, friendships and church congregations. Church splits and division are heartbreaking to individuals and I am sure it makes God sad.

Our churches should be places of relationships. These relationships are between people and the Lord. When we have a relationship with God, we allow His love to come into us and through us to others. When we are full of God, we overflow into the lives of others. Jesus had great compassion of those in need. His love comes through us to meet the needs of the sick, the poor and those in prison. This and bringing people to Christ is the mission of the Church. We love God and we love and help people.

Both Abraham and Moses were friends of God. (Genesis 18:1-8, Exodus 33:11 and James 2:23). They discussed matters with God - a relationship where they talked, shared and listened.

> A man who has friends must be a friend, but there is a friend who stays nearer than a brother. (Proverbs 18:24 NLT)

Our friendship with God is greater than the relationship we have with our families.

Friends are more than people we know, just met or are a casual acquaintance. I would say that my friends at church are more like family. We have a common bond of a relationship with God. We believe the scriptures, we pray, we show friendship and we are saved. We are the Church, the family of God.

Friendships are important. They make us complete. But having a friendship with God is the most important relationship in anyone's life. Knowing God is the highest goal and it is done through receiving Jesus Christ.

Chapter Questions

1. Find a scripture that tells you that the Church is the Body of Christ?

2. Righteousness comes by faith. How does someone become righteous in Christ?

3. How was Jesus one with Father? Please provide one scripture that shows Jesus' oneness with the Father.

4. Believers are the Family of God. Please explain briefly how believers are a family with God.

5. Find one scripture about the love of God. How does God demonstrate His love?

6. How does the love of God apply to the life of every believer?

7. Explain the difference between a social club and the church.

8. Write one fact about the Salvation Army.

9. What things would you do to help a young convert grow in the Lord?

10. Name two people in the Bible who were friends of God. What can a believer learn from these two people?

Chapter 10

A Relationship With God

It's plain and simple. A relationship with God - you need it today.

> For this is how God loved the world: He gave his one and only Son, so that everyone who believes in him will not perish but have eternal life. God sent his Son into the world not to judge the world, but to save the world through him. (John 3:16-17 NLT)

> I'm no longer calling you servants because servants don't understand what their master is thinking and planning. No, I've named you friends because I've let you in on everything I've heard from the Father. (John 15:15 MSG)

God wants you to come home to Him. It's a personal thing with Him because He loves you personally – He loves you as if you are the only person on earth.

Come to Him today. A relationship with God through receiving Jesus is only a few words away.

> Lord I need Jesus as my Lord and Savior. I believe that He died and rose from the dead. I receive you as my Lord and Master. Thank you, Jesus, for saving me.

If you sincerely prayed that prayer to God, the Bible says that you are now a believer. Welcome to the family of God. Read your Bible and talk to God. Find a local church that teaches the Bible and tell them you received Jesus Christ as you Lord and Savior. Attend as often as the doors are open and grow in God.

About the Author

Jeffrey lives in Virginia with his wonderful wife Sarah. They have two adult sons, Rob and Sam. Jeffrey taught the sciences in the public schools of Virginia as well as China and Jordan. He plays the bass guitar in the church music ministry and works with the prayer ministry.

He has taught the Bible on mission trips to the West African nations of Ivory Coast, Benin and Mali. Teaching the Bible to young man and women allows him to help them grow in their callings and ministries. This is Jeffrey's second book.

Please be sure to visit Amazon to see his first book, *The Kingdom of Heaven*.

He hopes that you enjoy reading *A Strong Relationship With God*.

PLEASE share this book with someone. THANKS!